Being of Sound Mind

A Play

Brian J. Burton

Samuel French - London
New York - Sydney - Toronto - Hollywood

Copyright © 1981 by Brian J.Burton
All Rights Reserved

BEING OF SOUND MIND is fully protected under the copyright laws of the British Commonwealth, including Canada, the United States of America, and all other countries of the Copyright Union. All rights, including professional and amateur stage productions, recitation, lecturing, public reading, motion picture, radio broadcasting, television and the rights of translation into foreign languages are strictly reserved.

ISBN 978-0-573-11022-1

www.samuelfrench-london.co.uk

www.samuelfrench.com

FOR AMATEUR PRODUCTION ENQUIRIES

UNITED KINGDOM AND WORLD EXCLUDING NORTH AMERICA
plays@SamuelFrench-London.co.uk
020 7255 4302/01

Each title is subject to availability from Samuel French,

depending upon country of performance.

CAUTION: Professional and amateur producers are hereby warned that BEING OF SOUND MIND is subject to a licensing fee. Publication of this play does not imply availability for performance. Both amateurs and professionals considering a production are strongly advised to apply to the appropriate agent before starting rehearsals, advertising, or booking a theatre. A licensing fee must be paid whether the title is presented for charity or gain and whether or not admission is charged.

The professional rights in this play are controlled by Samuel French Ltd, 52 Fitzroy Street, London, W1T 5JR

No one shall make any changes in this title for the purpose of production. No part of this book may be reproduced, stored in a retrieval system, or transmitted in any form, by any means, now known or yet to be invented, including mechanical, electronic, photocopying, recording, videotaping, or otherwise, without the prior written permission of the publisher. No one shall upload this title, or part of this title, to any social media websites.

The right of Brian J.Burton to be identified as author of this work has been asserted by him in accordance with Section 77 of the Copyright, Designs and Patents Act 1988.

CHARACTERS

John Pearson
Susan Pearson
Mrs March
A Man
Judy Farmer

The action takes place in the kitchen of a farmhouse in the Dordogne area of France

Time—the present

ACT I   Late afternoon in May
ACT II   Four hours later
ACT III 8.30 a.m. the next morning

ACT I

The kitchen of a farmhouse in the Dordogne area of France. Late afternoon in May. Saturday

There is a large rectangular kitchen table C *covered with a red check cloth and set at a slight angle to the audience. There are two upright wooden chairs above it and one at each end. There is a window with a wide ledge on the back wall* UR. *There is a pile of newspapers on the window-ledge. The window and the shutters are closed.* L *of the window is a large dresser with cupboards underneath. On the dresser are plates, bowls, cups and glasses.* UL *is a door which leads directly to the outside of the house. Below the door, on the same wall, are a refrigerator, a Calor gas stove, a sink with a draining-board on the downstage end and a cupboard at about the same height as the sink. A long case clock stands in the* UR *corner. On the centre of the* R *wall is a stone fireplace with a mantelshelf. On the mantelshelf are two gaudy ornaments and a large stuffed black cat. Below the fireplace is the door which leads to the bedrooms. Below the door on the same wall is a low cupboard. On top of the cupboard are an empty flower vase, a pile of paperbacks, a nondescript photograph in a frame, an ashtray and a brown jug. There are various pictures on the walls, mainly cheap prints of well-known paintings*

When the CURTAIN *rises, the room is in semi-darkness. The clock strikes five and, almost at once, voices are heard off* L *and the sound of a key being turned in the lock. The door* UL *opens and the light through the door increases the level in the room*

John Pearson enters first. He is a man in his early forties. He is wearing a sports coat and light trousers. He pushes the door open with his elbow as he is carrying two suitcases. He dumps the cases down by the dresser and then goes to open the windows and the shutters. He is followed into the room by his wife, Susan, who is carrying a holdall and a large plastic carrier of groceries. She is an attractive, dark-haired, highly-strung woman in her middle thirties. She is wearing a sweater and jeans. She puts the holdall alongside the suitcases and then moves to the table to put the carrier-bag down

John (*turning to face Susan*) Do you remember how this window opens? It appears to be stuck.
Susan It opens the same way as the one in the big bedroom.
John (*lightly*) Thank you. That's a lot of help, I must say.
Susan Isn't there a handle of some sort, in the middle, you have to turn?
John That's exactly what I'm trying to do but I'm not having much success.

Susan (*moving up to him*) Are you sure you're turning it in the right direction?
John Of course I—no, you're right. I'm not. That's it. (*He turns the handle and opens the windows inwards and then pushes the shutters outwards*) There we are, then.

The Lights increase as the room is bathed in evening sunshine

(*Looking round the room*) Well, here we are again. It all looks very much the same, doesn't it? Nothing seems to have altered since we were here last.
Susan (*moving* C) It smells a bit musty, doesn't it? I'd leave those windows open for a bit, if I was you.
John Good idea—I will. It's a nice evening anyway—quite warm. (*He rubs his hands*) I think we could be in for a spell of good weather.
Susan (*smiling*) As you've been repeating with sickening regularity ever since we got off the ferry. We'll have to hope that your amateur weather forecasting is more reliable than the media's.
John You know, you're quite right. It does smell a bit damp.
Susan Not surprising really. It's probably not had a fire in it all winter. We must be the first people who've used the place this year.
John What makes you say that?
Susan Being a week earlier than we were last year.
John Are we? I hadn't realized. Yes, I suppose we are. (*He flops down in one of the upright chairs*) God, I feel tired. I could do with a good old English armchair right now. That's one of the drawbacks of this place. The French must have tough posteriors, that's all I can say. Yes, I certainly feel weary. I felt O.K. until we arrived. Now I'm starting to feel the effects of all that driving I've done in the past two days. I don't mind telling you, I feel shattered. I never will understand those folk who drive all the way down from Cherbourg in one go. There can't be any pleasure in it. It must take the best part of the first week to recover and most of the second getting up the energy to drive back.
Susan You should have let me do my share of the driving, John. You can't say I didn't offer.
John I know you did. I didn't want you to, that's all.
Susan But why, John? Why wouldn't you? I kept asking you why but you wouldn't tell me. Don't you trust my driving—is that it?
John You know I do. Normally, you're a very good driver.
Susan Normally?
John You know what I mean.
Susan But I don't know, John. Tell me.
John I just want you to have as much rest as possible—that's all. You're not fully recovered yet, Susan.
Susan Oh, that's it, is it? You don't have to worry about that. (*She takes the carrier to the cupboard* DL) I'm fine, John. I really am. I keep telling you that. (*She starts to unpack some of the groceries and stack them into the cupboard*) It's ages since I felt as well as I do now.
John All the same, I'd much rather you took things fairly easy for a while longer. There's no point in asking for trouble, is there?

Act I

Susan (*as she puts away the groceries*) What sort of trouble would that be, John?
John You know very well what sort of trouble I mean. You just have to face the fact that it's going to take time. You can't expect to recover from anything as serious as that in five minutes. The psychiatrist told me that—
Susan (*turning to face him*) For Christ's sake, John—don't fuss. You're just like an old woman, sometimes, the way you go on.
John Thank you. Thank you very much indeed.
Susan I'm sorry, John, but you are.
John Look—don't let's quarrel as soon as we get here.
Susan Come off it, John—be fair. You started it with your hinting.
John I don't think I did but that's beside the point.
Susan A fine sort of holiday we're going to have if you're going to gently remind me every five minutes that I spent two months in a mental hospital. Can't we leave it at that?
John O.K. O.K. It suits me. Just as long as you know what you're doing.
Susan I know what I'm doing all right—believe me. It's all over. It's in the past. It's never likely to happen again.
John Well, let's hope you're right. I wouldn't be so sure though, if I was you.
Susan Why should it happen again? You know very well, I've never suffered from anything like that before, have I? (*She pauses*) Why don't you answer me, John?
John I think you know the reason.
Susan But I don't. Answer me, John—please. If there's something you want to say, for God's sake say it and let's be finished with it once and for all.
John Very well. I'll give you your answer but only because you're forcing me to. Don't blame me if you don't like it.
Susan Go on.
John Why do you think your father put that absurd condition into his will?
Susan Oh, not that again. How the hell should I know? (*She moves up stage towards him*) John, we've been over and over that God knows how many times in the past nine months. Why bring it up again?
John I didn't want to.
Susan Like hell, you didn't. It's an obsession with you. I don't want to talk about it again—do you hear?
John There is absolutely no point at all in behaving like an ostrich, Susan. You just have to face facts. There was a history of mental illness in your family. What's the point of denying it?
Susan Who's denying it? I'm not. My mother's last few years before she died were spent in a mental home. You know damn well they were. But that is it, as far as I know. There's been no other history of mental illness in the family, as you so delicately put it. How many more times do I have to tell you? (*She moves away DL and angrily resumes unpacking the carrier*)

John All right—all right. Forget it.
Susan Don't worry. I intend to. I'm not letting it ruin our holiday. (*More calmly*) I'll just finish putting these groceries away and then I'll give you a hand with the rest of the stuff from the car. (*Turning to him*) Sorry I shouted at you, John. I must admit, you do look tired. You sit there and have a rest for a few minutes. (*She moves up to him and kisses him lightly on the cheek*) Friends again?
John Of course.
Susan And thank you for doing the driving.
John That's all right. I'll soon recover. Be back on top form tomorrow, you'll see. We'll get the badminton net up and so on.
Susan Great.
John (*after a pause*) It was odd about the Duvals, wasn't it?
Susan (*moving to the sink*) Very. Very odd indeed. (*She gets out washing-up liquid and cleaning cloths from the cupboard under the sink*)
John They've always been there to give us the keys before.
Susan Exactly.
John I can't get over the way they left the keys in that envelope stuck in the door. Anyone could have taken them.
Susan (*getting out a plastic bowl*) Oh, I don't know. I wouldn't say it was much of a risk. I very much doubt if this area is heavily populated with criminal types lurking in the shadows waiting to swipe house keys. Anyway, with no address on the envelope, they'd have to try quite a few houses before they found the right one.
John That's true.
Susan Anyway, it's not the easiest of places to find, is it? It took us long enough the first time we came here, didn't it—even after the Duvals gave us directions?
John Did it? I don't remember.
Susan Of course you do. We drove round and round in circles looking for the wretched place. You don't remember because you don't want to admit you have no sense of direction. That's what it is.
John It would have helped if the place had a name.
Susan What—the French equivalent of "Dunromin", you mean?
John Something like that.
Susan So you do remember?
John Yes, I suppose so. (*He pauses*) All the same, I do think the Duvals should have been there when we arrived. I suppose you did fill in the card the agents gave us to say what time we were arriving, did you?
Susan Of course. I posted it more than three weeks ago just to be on the safe side as the post is so slow in this part of the world.
John They must have known, then.
Susan I expect they've gone into Ribérac to do some shopping or something as it's Whitsun week-end. (*She wipes the draining-board*) The draining-board and sink look as though nobody's washed them in months.
John The rest of the place looks O.K. though. Someone must have cleaned it fairly recently.

Act I

Susan We'll pop out this evening later on, if you feel like it, and see if they're back. I'd hate to miss the opportunity of catching up on the local gossip.

John It's all right for you; your French is much better than mine. Half the time, I just stand there like a lemon without a clue of what you're chuntering on about.

Susan You really ought to try and do something about your awful schoolboy French, John, now that you're spending so much time on the Continent.

John I don't have any trouble. I get by fine. The sort of people I go and see all speak English anyway and they like the opportunity to air it.

Susan The Englishman's standard excuse for not bothering to learn another language. We ought to be downright ashamed of ourselves.

John I suppose so. (*He rises and moves to the fireplace*) God, these ghastly ornaments! Nobody's broken them since we were here last year, I see.

Susan No such luck. They really are dreadful, aren't they?

John Shall I put them in the cupboard as usual?

Susan Please. (*She turns towards the fireplace*) Oh God, that blasted Satan is sitting there as sinister and ugly as ever. Put the damn thing out of sight, will you? (*She shudders*) I hate cats anyway but that thing really gives me nightmares.

John I know. I'll put it in the barn, if you like—out of the way altogether.

Susan No, don't bother to do that. Just as long as it's in the cupboard and not sitting on the mantelshelf grinning at me. Ugh! (*She switches on the fridge and starts to put the milk and butter away*)

John (*picking up the ornaments and the cat*) I wonder if all the other people who stay here do the same.

Susan Put the ornaments and the cat away in the cupboard, do you mean?

John Yes.

Susan I wonder. It'd be fascinating to find out. Perhaps they do. Who knows, it could be that the only time Satan and Co. see the light of day is in the winter and on alternate Saturday mornings in the summer season.

John (*moving to the cupboard* DR) Interesting thought. (*He opens the cupboard door and puts the ornaments inside*) Right, Satan my lad, that's where you're going to live for the next two weeks. And I'm warning you, no howling for Kit-e-Kat in the middle of the night.

Susan Don't, John—please.

John (*straightening up*) Don't what?

Susan Go on about that bloody cat—please.

John Sorry—I was only joking.

Susan I know you were but I don't find it amusing. It really does frighten me—honestly.

John O.K. Point taken. I'll go and get the rest of the luggage out of the car. I'll put the loungers and the badminton stuff in the barn. We don't want to clutter up the house with them.

Susan Right—I'll be with you in a minute. I'll just turn on the gas bottles. I hope they're not empty—they've got to last us until Tuesday. (*She opens the door under the sink and kneels to turn on the gas bottles*)

John I'm sure the Duvals will have checked them to see they're O.K. Look. I can manage the rest of the things on my own. (*He goes to the door* UL) I wouldn't mind a cup of coffee though. Do you think you could rustle one up?
Susan Sure. The gas seems all right. I'll put the water on.
John Good.

John exits L

Susan moves to the dresser and takes a small green saucepan and coffee-pot from the bottom cupboard. She takes them to the stove, fills the saucepan with water, lights the gas with a match and puts the saucepan on to the ring

John enters with another suitcase and a portable radio. He crosses above the table, leaves the radio on the table, picks up one of the suitcases from by the dresser and goes through the door DR *to the bedrooms*

Susan collects cups, saucers and spoons from the dresser and puts them on the draining-board. She takes a jar of coffee from the cupboard DL *and starts to prepare the coffee*

John enters from R *and collects the other suitcase and the holdall*

John I've put them in the big room as usual, is that O.K.?
Susan Of course. You weren't thinking of sleeping on your own, were you?
John Well, I didn't know. I mean, we haven't . . .
Susan Leave them where they are, John.
John Right.
Susan I'll unpack them later.
John No hurry. Just relax for a while. I'm certainly going to when I've dumped these. How's the coffee going?
Susan Fine. Be ready in a minute. Just waiting for the water to boil. It takes ages in a saucepan. I can't imagine why the French don't use kettles.
John No rush.

John exits R *with the suitcase and holdall*

Susan (*calling*) Anything changed in there?
John (*off*) Doesn't look like it, as far as I can see. Still the same lumpy mattress, I'm afraid.

John enters R

You really would think the owner would do something about it, wouldn't you?
Susan Perhaps nobody's complained. We certainly can't talk. We didn't. We always said we would, every year, but we never got round to it, did we?
John It didn't seem very important when we were back home. I suppose that's the reason. (*He goes to the window and looks out*)
Susan Perhaps we ought to do something about it this year if only for the sake of the other visitors. I tell you what, we'll have a word with the

Act I

Duvals. They could contact the owners and see if they could come up with something better. What do you think, shall we mention it to the Duvals?

John You can do if you like but I don't suppose they can do much about it.

Susan Why do you say that?

John I understand the owner lives in England.

Susan Does he? How do you know that? I didn't know.

John (*turning to face her*) I thought the Duvals told us.

Susan When? They didn't tell me. I've never spoken to them about the owner.

John I must have been mistaken. I thought they had. (*He sits at the table*) That's all the stuff out of the car apart from what's going in the barn. I'll see to that after I've had my coffee.

Susan (*as she pours the coffee*) Fine. It's only instant. Is that all right? I'll grind some beans later.

John Suits me fine.

Susan (*moving to the table with two cups of coffee*) Here you are, then.

John Great—thank you.

Susan (*sitting down*) I think we've enough food for the long week-end. We'll go into Riberac in the morning. There's sure to be some shops open even though it's Whit Sunday. The *boulangerie* is bound to be open. I can't see the French going without their fresh bread.

John Don't worry. We'll manage even if the shops aren't open. Anyway, I'm not particularly bothered about food at present.

Susan I'm not at all surprised. That was quite a lunch we had today.

John I can't resist French food, particularly if there's *fruits de mer* on the menu; you know me.

Susan I should do after ten years.

John (*stretching*) Ah—*c'est la vie!* (*He pauses*) What do you say?

Susan Just think—two whole weeks with nothing to do. Just the two of us on our own. Nobody can get in touch with us, come hell or high water. You didn't give them this address at the bank, did you?

John Not on your life. If the Foreign Department can't manage for two weeks without getting in touch with me when they've got problems it's a pretty poor set-up. That's what I say.

Susan Hear, hear!

John We don't have to do anything at all if we don't want to and we don't have to go anywhere—just laze around in the sun. That's what I call a holiday.

Susan Suits me fine. (*She pauses*) But what about going to see Judy in Bordeaux? We'll have to go there at least. We always do when we're down here.

John We'll see. We'll see.

Susan Whatever else we do or don't do, I really think we ought to make the effort to go and see her. She'd be terribly disappointed if we didn't go.

John I said, we'd see. Don't let's make any definite plans to do anything, Susan.

Susan You don't like Judy, do you, John?

John Why, in heaven's name, do you ask that all of a sudden?
Susan I don't really know—just a feeling. You don't, do you?
John Your sister's fine—in small doses. I've no very strong feelings about her one way or the other, to tell you the truth.
Susan If we do go and see her, try and make an effort to be nice, won't you?
John Why this sudden concern for Judy? At any other time, you've hardly a good word to say for her, have you?
Susan I know, but she must be feeling pretty upset about the will. She must have been reckoning on getting something. I still don't understand why Father treated her like that.
John You know what I think, don't you?
Susan That Father wasn't over-fond of Martin. I know—but that shouldn't have made any difference. Anyway, Martin died more than a year before my father. He had plenty of time to change his will if he wanted to.
John Perhaps he thought Martin had left her fairly well-off anyway. It was a pretty good job he had with that wine firm.
Susan But that's hardly the point, is it?
John I suppose not.
Susan Talking of money, how many travellers cheques did you cash at that hotel in Limoges this morning?
John Not many. You know you don't get a very good rate of exchange in a hotel. I just cashed enough to keep us going until the banks re-open on Tuesday.
Susan I see. That's all right then.
John (*after a pause*) God, I've just thought of something. (*He rises*)
Susan What?
John After I'd cashed the cheques, you called me to help with the cases, didn't you?
Susan Did I? Yes, I think I did. Why?
John I don't remember picking my passport up off the desk. I think I must have left it behind.
Susan I'm sure you picked it up.
John Why do you say that? Did you see me?
Susan Well, no, I don't think I did but you must have done—surely.
John I really don't think so (*He feels in his inside pocket*) It's not here.
Susan Didn't you put it back into your travel wallet?
John No—no, I'm certain I didn't.
Susan (*rising*) I'll go and have a look. Where is your wallet?
John On the bed. I'll go and have a look in the car to see if, by any chance, I dropped it.

John exits L

> *Susan exits* R *into the bedroom and returns with a leather zip document case. She sits at the table, opens the case and looks at each pocket in turn. She takes out a passport and a pocket wallet, puts them on the table and continues her search. She takes out two or three airline tickets and some*

Act I 9

other papers. She stops and examines the tickets, looking puzzled. She is still looking at them when John is heard returning UL. *She puts all the papers and the passport back into the case and zips it up*

John enters L

(*As he enters*) It's not in the car. Was it in the case?
Susan What did you say? No—no, no, your passport's not here—only mine.
John Damn! Damn! Damn! It's a good two-hour's drive to Limoges. I think I'll give them a ring first to see if they've found it. I noticed when we drove up this lane that they've put a coin box outside that *bar tabac* on the corner.
Susan Finish your coffee first, John. We'll have another search for it in a minute. You might have dropped it on the grass when you were unloading the car.
John Not much chance of that, I'm afraid. No, I'm positive I left it at that hotel. I'll have to see if I can find their phone number.
Susan It'll be in the *Michelin*. If you like, I'll come up to the phone box and do the talking.
John Don't bother; I can manage.
Susan Well, let's hope it is there. If it is, you won't have to dash up there tonight, will you? You won't need it till Tuesday.
John That's true. (*He sits down*) It's not like me to do a stupid thing like that. God, this is a fine start to our holiday, isn't it?
Susan Don't worry, John. We're bound to get it back—but even if we don't, it isn't exactly the end of the world, is it?
John I know that, but it would be a wretched nuisance. A chap at the bank lost his passport in Spain and he—

There is a knock at the door UL

Mrs March (*off*) Anyone at home?
John (*to Susan; quietly*) Who the hell's that?
Susan No idea; you'd better go and see.
John (*rising and calling*) Just a minute. (*He goes to the door* UL *and opens it*) Yes?
Mrs March (*off*) Look, I'm really sorry to disturb you good folks. The name is March—Mrs March. May I come in for a moment? I won't keep you long, I promise.
John Of course; come on in. We're just here in the kitchen. It's straight through.
Mrs March (*off*) Yes, I do know my way, thank you.

Mrs March enters. She is a smartly dressed woman in her mid-thirties. She carries a handbag and speaks with a slight Australian accent

Mrs March Sorry to barge in on you like this.
Susan Not at all. Do sit down, please.
Mrs March Oh, thank you. (*She sits down*)

John sits on her left

Susan We were just having some coffee. Can I get you a cup? (*She rises*)
Mrs March Please don't go to any trouble on my account.
Susan No trouble at all—really.
Mrs March Right—in that case, I reckon I'll join you.
Susan (*going to the dresser for a cup and saucer*) It's only instant, I'm afraid. (*She moves down to the stove*)
Mrs March No worries—suits me fine. I mustn't stay, though. I just popped in to see if everything was O.K.
John In what way?
Mrs March Oh, I'm sorry—what must you be thinking? I didn't say who I was, did I? I'm the owner of this little place.
Susan The owner?
Mrs March That's right. You don't have to sound so surprised.
Susan Did I? I'm sorry. (*She lights the gas and puts more water on to boil*) It's just that I thought—or that is, my husband thought the owner lived in England.
Mrs March I do. I don't live in Australia if that's what you're thinking. I'll tell you that for nothing. I used to live there—I was born there in fact—but I married a Pom and I've lived in England ever since.
Susan I see.
Mrs March I stay here—in this house—sometimes in the late Spring but most of the time it's let to visitors, like you folk. Well now, I'd better tell you why I called, hadn't I? You see, I didn't reckon there'd be anyone here this week and then the agents rang up to say they'd let it and I was a bit anxious in case Monsieur and Madame Duval hadn't been told and the place hadn't been cleaned up and so on. The Duvals aren't on the phone so I reckoned the only thing to do was to come and find out for myself. So, I caught a plane to Bordeaux, hired a car and here I am.
John That was extremely kind of you.
Mrs March No problem, no problem at all—my pleasure.
Susan (*pouring coffee*) Yes, it was very thoughtful of you.
Mrs March Don't say another word about it.
Susan Do you take sugar in your coffee?
Mrs March No—no sugar—no milk—just as it comes. I used to take a slice of lemon, years ago, but folks in the U.K. don't drink it that way so I gave it away. You know, when in Rome and so on.
Susan (*giving coffee to Mrs March*) Here it is then. You can have some lemon if you like.
Mrs March No thank you, dear. This is beaut.
Susan Right. (*She sits down*)
Mrs March (*looking round the room*) Well now. You're here and everything looks fair dinkum so I needn't have bothered. All the same, I'm glad I did. I'd have been worried all the week if I hadn't, my word I would. Right—so I'll just drink my coffee and then I'll stroll round and see the Duvals and—
John They're not there—at least they weren't when we arrived about a half an hour ago.

Act I

Mrs March Not there? How did you get the keys, then?
Susan They left them in an envelope stuck in the door.
Mrs March Did they now? Oh well, that's it then—no point in going round there. (*She drinks her coffee*) Have you been to this part of France before?
Susan Oh yes—several times. This is the third year running we've stayed in this house. We love it, don't we, John?
John It's exactly right for the sort of relaxing holiday we like.
Mrs March You say you've stayed here three times?
Susan Didn't you know?
Mrs March No—no. I leave all the bookings to the agents. I rarely get to know the names of the visitors.
John Oh, forgive me—you must think me frightfully rude. I forgot to introduce ourselves. I'm John Pearson and this is my wife, Susan.
Mrs March Glad to know you, Susan, John. My name's March—Mrs March. If I tell you my first name, you must promise not to laugh.
John Why should we laugh?
Mrs March I had no problem until I go and get myself married to this man called March. You see, my first name is April. April March—get it? I ask you! It almost put me off getting married to Tom, my word it did.
Susan Well, I think it's a very nice name, Mrs March.
Mrs March You don't have to live with it, dear.
Susan Yes, I see what you mean. (*She pauses*) Are you staying in Bordeaux?
Mrs March No, I've booked into a little hotel in Ribérac. I'm catching a plane back to England in the morning. As I said, I only just dashed over to see if everything was fixed up.
John It really was very considerate of you. I'm extremely grateful.
Susan It was most thoughtful.
Mrs March It was the very least I could do in the circumstances. You see, I usually only let the place from the first week in June but there was this mix up with the agents.
John I think, April, you—
Susan But we stayed here in May last year, didn't we, John?
John May? No, I don't think we did. You must have forgotten.
Susan But we did, John.
John I'm sorry, Susan but you're mistaken. It wasn't in May.
Susan It was, John. It was the week after my father died, don't you remember? It must have been May.
John Look, it isn't important. Leave it, Susan. You're getting things mixed up again.
Susan But I—oh, it doesn't matter anyway.
John No, it doesn't matter at all.
Susan Whereabouts in England do you live, Mrs March?
Mrs March Me? I live in a little place in Kent.
Susan Oh, yes—whereabouts in Kent?
Mrs March Hythe. I don't suppose you know it.

Susan Oh but I do—a little. I went there for a long week-end about two years ago. I went with an old schoolfriend of mine.
Mrs March Did you now? Of course, we don't live in Hythe itself. It's a few miles outside—just a small village.
Susan It's charming round there.
Mrs March We like it.
Susan What does your husband do?
Mrs March Do, dear?
Susan For a living.
Mrs March He's a consultant.
Susan Really? He's a doctor, is he?
Mrs March Oh my word no. Nothing like that. He advises folks who want to take out insurances.
Susan He must travel about quite a lot.
Mrs March Oh, yes, he does.
Susan And do you work?
Mrs March No, I don't work. I live the life of a lady of leisure. I used to work, of course. I was a hairdresser until I met Tom. I came to the U.K. about—
John Would you like a drink, April? I haven't opened the duty free yet.
Mrs March Well now, let me see. I—all right, why not? Thank you, I will.
John (*rising*) It's in the bedroom. I'll go and get it. I won't be a tick.

John exits R

Susan (*rising and going to the dresser*) Have you any family, Mrs March?
Mrs March No—no family. Have you?
Susan (*taking three glasses, one with red grapes painted on it, from the dresser*) Unfortunately, no. There's just John and me.
Mrs March Been married long, have you, Susan?
Susan (*moving to the table and sitting down*) Ten years.
Mrs March Fifteen me. I was only eighteen when I married Tom. The old April March joke's wearing a bit thin by now, I can tell you.

John enters R, a bottle of whisky in one hand and a bottle of brandy in the other

John Here we are then. Duty free whisky and cognac. Not that they are duty free exactly. They must make a fortune out of selling booze on the ferries. I read somewhere that it's one of their main sources of income. Now then—what's it to be—whisky or brandy?
Mrs March Brandy for me, please.
John Right. (*He puts the whisky bottle on the dresser and moves back to the table to open the brandy*)
Mrs March You wouldn't happen to have any ice, would you?
John I doubt it. Have we, Susan?
Susan No, I'm sorry. I've only just turned on the fridge. Being the first people here this year, you see, there—
Mrs March Oh, yes—of course, I forgot. No worries—I'll have it straight up.

Act I

John (*pouring a large measure of brandy and passing it to Mrs March*) Here you are then.

Mrs March Oh my word, that's a bit on the large side, isn't it?

John It's a special occasion, isn't it? (*He pours two more drinks from the same bottle*) Not every day one meets the owner, is it? (*He hands the decorated glass to Susan and sits*) It's strange really. We've stayed here so often we've begun to refer to the place as though it was our own.

Mrs March Well now, I take that as a compliment. I like to think of people feeling at home here. (*She looks round the room*) It's not much really—the house I mean. It's in a great area and very secluded but it's pretty basic—the furniture and so on. I bought most of it from the previous owners—local people. They were not exactly overflowing with good taste.

John It's fine. It really is.

Susan There is one thing though, if you don't mind me mentioning it. We were saying, just before you arrived, that we ought to get in touch with the owners. You see, it's the—

John Not now, Susan.

Susan But we said that if—

John Not now, please.

Susan Oh, very well.

Mrs March (*rising suddenly and moving to the fireplace*) Don't tell me somebody's pinched those bloody ornaments off the mantelpiece.

Susan Well, no—the fact is . . .

Mrs March (*turning to face* C) You've hidden them away somewhere—is that it?

Susan Well, yes—you see . . .

Mrs March (*moving back to the table*) Look, dear—you don't have to apologize. I hate the bloody things. I always hide them away when I'm staying here. (*She sits down*)

Susan You do? That's a relief, I must say.

Mrs March Tell you the truth, I wish somebody would pinch them or break them or something. I can't imagine how I came to leave them there in the first place. Oh—where's Satan? He ought to be up there on the mantelpiece. That's where he lives.

Susan Not when we're here, he doesn't.

Mrs March Why ever not? Don't you like stuffed cats?

Susan It's not just stuffed cats, it's cats in general—stuffed or otherwise.

Mrs March Really? What is it, do they frighten you or something?

Susan It's more than that. I couldn't begin to describe to you the effect they have on me. Some people feel that way about snakes—with me it's cats. They make the hair stand up on the back of my neck—literally.

Mrs March Oh my word. Well, Satan had better stay where he is, then.

Susan I'm afraid so—sorry.

Mrs March That's all right, Susan. You don't have to apologize. Look, I'll take him away with me if you like.

John No—no. We don't want to put you to any trouble. Just so long as it's where Susan can't see it—that's all. (*He pours more brandy in Mrs March's glass*) Drop more?

Mrs March It looks as though you've made up my mind for me, John. Well, thanks, I will.

John pours another drink for himself and Susan

Right, then—let's drink to your holiday.

John Nice thought—thank you.

Susan I expect you know this area fairly well.

Mrs March Should do—I've spent a lot of time here.

Susan You probably know some good places to eat. We've been to quite a few but we're always interested in somewhere different.

Mrs March Well now, let me think.

John (*to Susan*) We know enough places, Susan. I'm sure April doesn't want to have to—

Mrs March Why not? Be glad to. What sort of restaurants do you like?

Susan John's particular love is seafood.

Mrs March Seafood—let me think now. If this was Sydney it'd be no problem. That's one of the things I miss in this part of the world—those beautiful rock oysters. Now then, let me see . . .

John Look—don't worry—please. We know lots of places.

Mrs March There are a couple of good restaurants in the village but I expect you've been to those.

Susan Oh yes—and to that *Routier* place by the bridge. I can't think of its name at the moment, can you, John?

John No, I don't think I can.

Susan (*to Mrs March*) You must know it. What's it called?

Mrs March Do you know, it's gone right out of my head. I'm pretty hopeless about names anyway—always have been. I eat in a lot when I'm staying here. I usually go to the market in Ribérac, on a Thursday, and stock up with goodies to last me for the rest of the week.

Susan But the—I see.

John Nothing quite like good home-cooked food I always say.

Susan Since when? You always want to eat out when we're on holiday.

John Yes—well—I mean, no point in coming away on holiday to slave over the kitcken sink, is there?

Mrs March I really must be going shortly and leave you two to get on with your holiday. I've taken up enough of your time already.

John Look—no need to hurry off. Have another drink?

Mrs March Well—I really shouldn't but I will all the same. Brandy's one of my weaknesses.

John (*pouring drinks*) I've just had an idea. There's no point in you going back to spend a solitary evening in a hotel. Why not stay and have a meal with us? We picked up some groceries in Limoges. I'm sure Susan can rustle up a meal, can't you?

Susan Yes—yes, of course. It would be a pleasure. Talking of Limoges, what about that phone call we were going to make to the hotel?

Act I

John Don't worry. I'll ring them later.
Susan I'm not worrying. You were the one who was getting all upset.
Mrs March Don't put yourselves out on my account, please. I'm fine. I don't mind going back to the hotel. I don't want to be a nuisance.
John No nuisance—no nuisance at all, I promise you. We'd be delighted if you stayed. After all, you've gone to a great deal of trouble on our behalf. The least we can do is—
Mrs March No—I'll go. I've got to get that flight from Bordeaux at eleven fifteen in the morning. I'd appreciate an early night.
John I—I . . .
Mrs March No arguments—I've decided. I'll just stay and finish my drink. (*She opens her handbag*) Damn!
John Something wrong?
Mrs March No—not really. It's just that I've left my ciggies at the hotel, that's all.
Susan I'm sorry. We can't help—neither of us smokes.
Mrs March Very wise too. I wish I could give it away. I've tried a number of times but I just don't seem to have sufficient will power or whatever it takes.
John If I'd known, I'd have bought some duty free but with neither of us smoking . . .
Mrs March Look—no worries. I'll have to do without until I get back to the hotel. It'll do me good. I haven't had a smoke since I left there so I'm sure I can wait a few minutes longer. It's a stupid habit. The trouble is that you never want a ciggy so much as when you haven't got one.
John I've got an idea. I have to go up the lane to the call box. It's outside the *café tabac*. I'll go now and bring you back some cigarettes.
Mrs March Not on your life, you won't. No—really, it's not that important. Anyway, I can call in there on my way back to the hotel.
John (*rising*) I insist. It's no trouble at all. (*He moves to the door* UL) You stay and finish your drink. I doubt if I'll be more than five minutes at the outside.
Susan (*rising and moving towards John*) Can you manage the phone call on your own?
John I reckon so. It's pretty straightforward.
Susan Right—you get off, then. I can have a chat with Mrs March while you're away.
John Fine. Won't be long.
Mrs March It's very good of you. You make me feel terribly guilty.
John Not at all. Any particular brand of cigarette? I don't know one from the other, I'm afraid.
Mrs March I prefer American "if they stock them" but it doesn't matter—any kind will do.
John (*as he goes*) I'll see what they've got, then. Back in a few minutes.

John exits L

Susan moves back to the table and sits down

Mrs March Your husband is very kind. He shouldn't have bothered. I could have managed without.

There is the sound of a car starting up and driving away, off

Susan John won't mind—really.

Mrs March That's all right then. (*She pauses*) Well, it looks as though you could be in for a good spell of weather. I hope so, anyway for your sakes. I expect you've been looking forward to your holiday.

Susan Yes—I have, particularly. I can certainly do with it. I've not been too well lately.

Mrs March Oh, I'm sorry to hear that. Anything serious?

Susan Yes. I've had a pretty rough time.

Mrs March What sort of rough time? Oh, I'm sorry—that's rude of me. I shouldn't ask questions like that. I didn't intend to pry. I'm just interested, you know.

Susan That's all right. There's no need to apologize. I don't mind telling you. I can talk about it now. I certainly couldn't have done a couple of months ago. Things got on top of me. I had a miscarriage, you see, and I was quite ill afterwards.

Mrs March I'm sorry. I wouldn't have asked if I'd . . .

Susan Don't worry. It's all right. It really is. After all, thousands of women have miscarriages every day but the majority survive. It's just that, in my case, I went to pieces.

Mrs March Very understandable.

Susan I just gave up completely. I had this terrible depression. I was incapable of looking after myself, let alone John. Everyone kept telling me I'd get over it—it was just a matter of time; but I didn't get over it—it got worse, far worse. My sister came to stay for a while—that was a help but she couldn't stay long; she had to get back to her job after a couple of weeks. They were short-staffed or something. She works in an airline office in Bordeaux.

Mrs March Does she, now?

Susan Yes—she's quite high-powered, by all accounts. Anyway, as I said, she had to go back. After she'd gone, I kept telling myself to snap out of it but it didn't help. It went from bad to worse. Finally, I reached a stage where I had to have treatment—you know.

Mrs March What sort of treatment?

Susan God, it was awful—awful. It was like a terrible nightmare. A minute or so ago, I said I could talk about it but when I start remembering the details, I don't think I can.

Mrs March Might help if you did. Get it out of your system—if you see what I mean.

Susan I suppose you're right. Perhaps it would.

Mrs March I'm quite certain it would.

Susan All right then. You see—they thought I was insane.

Mrs March Insane?

Susan Yes—they put me into a mental hospital.

Mrs March My word—that's awful! For long?

Act I

Susan I was in there for two months altogether.
Mrs March Two months, eh? As long as that? Oh well, never mind—could have been worse.
Susan Have you any idea of what it's like in a mental hospital?
Mrs March No—I can't say I have, dear. I've never had any trouble of that sort myself.
Susan You're lucky. Tell me, Mrs March, if I hadn't told you, would you have known?
Mrs March I don't think I follow you.
Susan Well, what I mean is—do I seem fairly normal to you? Do I?

Pause

Why don't you answer me, Mrs March?
Mrs March (*rising and moving away from the table*) I'd prefer not to, if you don't mind.
Susan Why not?
Mrs March Well—I always say it takes all sorts to make a world.
Susan I see. And what sort am I? Go on—answer me.
Mrs March (*turning to face Susan*) For God's sake, Susan, stop pushing me. I'm not qualified to pass any opinion on your mental condition. It's unfair to ask me, isn't it? On the other hand, I doubt very much if they'd have put you away for two months unless—unless . . .
Susan Unless what?
Mrs March Well, unless they were pretty certain you were a looney.
Susan (*rising*) What did you say? What did you call me?
Mrs March Look, dear, I'm sorry. I shouldn't have said that. It was tactless of me. Please forget it. Let's drop the subject, shall we? Let's talk about something else.
Susan You're deliberately trying to upset me, aren't you?
Mrs March Of course not—whatever gave you that idea? (*She moves towards Susan*) Now look, dear . . .
Susan You thought I was a looney, as you call it, as soon as you set eyes on me, didn't you?
Mrs March Don't be absurd.
Susan I'm not being absurd. I saw the look on your face when you found out about the cat. After all, no normal person would react to a stuffed cat like that, would they? No sane person would hide it away in a cupboard, would they? That's what you thought when we told you, wasn't it? (*More loudly*) Wasn't it? (*Shouting*) Wasn't it?
Mrs March All right—all right—I heard you the first time. There's no need to shout at me. I'm not deaf. Now, just calm down, for Christ's sake. There is no reason to get yourself all worked up like that.
Susan Right. (*She moves to the cupboard* DR) I'll show you if I'm mad. (*She opens the cupboard and takes out the cat*) Look, here's the cat—see. Now, watch—go on, watch! I'm holding it. I'm touching it—do you see? Do you? Now, look—I'm stroking it. I wouldn't do that if I was a looney, would I? Would I? (*Screaming*) Would I? Would I? (*More quietly*) Go on—say something. Don't just stand there staring at me.

Mrs March Look, Susan, I don't want you to try to prove anything to me. You don't have to—believe me. Put the bloody cat back into the cupboard, please.

Susan (*slowly*) I don't like you. I don't like you at all. There's something very strange about you. It's almost as though I've met you before somewhere—I don't know when. Perhaps it was just someone like you. I really don't know. You frighten me. I don't know why, but you frighten me. I think you are an evil woman.

Mrs March Well, I must say that—

Susan Here—take your blasted cat—take it and get out of here and leave us in peace. (*Shouting*) Do you hear me? Get out! Get out! Get out!

Mrs March (*taking the cat*) Very well, I'll go. If you want my opinion, I'll give it to you—free, gratis and for nothing. I'm not at all surprised they put you in the looney bin. The only thing I can't understand is why the hell they let you out again. It's obvious that you should still be in there. You may have had very good cause for being upset, you may have been ill, but there is not the slightest possible excuse for the abominable way you've just carried on. Please, tell your husband I'm sorry I had to go and that he went to get me the cigarettes for nothing. (*She opens her handbag*) Here's five francs, that should cover the cost. (*She slaps down the coins on the table*)

There is the sound of a car driving up and stopping, off

And I would suggest to you that when you start planning your next year's holiday, you look for somewhere else to stay. You'll not stay in my place again—my oath, you won't.

The door UL *opens and a Man walks in. He is of a similar build to John and dressed in almost identical clothes—but there the resemblance ends*

Man (*moving to the table*) I left my wallet on the table. I had to—what's the matter, April? Is something wrong?

Mrs March It's Susan. I'm afraid she's had some sort of attack—hysterics or something. I'd see if I could calm her down if I was you.

Man I see. What is it, Susan? What's happened? You haven't been having a row with April, have you?

Susan (*moving up to the table, facing upstage*) I don't understand. What are you talking about? Who are you?

Man What do you mean—who am I? I'm John, I'm your husband, of course.

Susan starts to scream hysterically as—

the CURTAIN *falls*

ACT II

The same. Four hours later

When the CURTAIN *rises, the room is in semi-darkness apart from the light streaming in from the bedroom through the open door. The windows are closed, but the shutters are still open. It is twilight outside. Susan is seated at the table. She is asleep with her head resting on her arms on the table. The clock strikes nine. There is a loud knocking on the door* UL. *Susan doesn't stir. The knocking is heard again, louder*

Judy (*off*) Is there anyone in? (*Knocking*) Susan, are you there? Susan!
Susan (*starting up*) Who is it? For God's sake, who is it? What do you want?
Judy (*off*) Susan, it's me—Judy. Let me in, please. Susan!
Susan Judy! Thank God! (*She rushes to the door* UL *and unbolts it*) Oh, Judy, thank God you've come. (*She opens the door*) Oh, Judy! Judy!

Judy enters and takes Susan into her arms. She is a young woman in her early thirties—very chic in the French style

Judy It's all right, Susan, it's all right. I'm here now.
Susan Oh, Judy, it's terrible—terrible. I don't know what to do. I just don't know what to do. Help me, Judy—help me. You will, won't you? Say you will.
Judy Come along, Susan, and sit down.

Judy leads Susan to the table

Sit down now.

Susan sits

That's better. Now calm down and tell me what it's all about. Take your time and try not to get too upset. It won't help.
Susan I don't know how to begin. I'm sure you won't believe me anyway.
Judy Don't be silly. I'm sure I'll believe you. Why shouldn't I? Just a minute—I'll put on the light and then we can see where we are. Where's the switch?
Susan By the front door.
Judy Right. (*She goes to the door* UL *and switches on the main light*)

The room becomes lighter

That's better. Now then. (*She goes back to the table and sits down*) I couldn't make out more than a word or two of what you were saying on the phone. Then your money ran out. I waited for a while in case you rang me back. When you didn't, I decided that the only thing to do was to get in the car and rush over here to find out what it was all about.

Susan I only had two francs. I tried to get you back through the operator but she didn't seem to understand. I was desperate. I didn't know what to do. Oh, Judy—you will help me, won't you?

Judy Don't get so upset, Susan. Of course, I'll help you if I can—you know that, but first of all I must know what it's all about. Where's John?

Susan I don't know, Judy. That's the whole point—I just don't know.

Judy What do you mean you don't know? He came with you, didn't he? You didn't come on holiday on your own, did you?

Susan Oh, no—I didn't come here on my own—of course I didn't. You didn't think I came here on my own, did you?

Judy I don't know, do I?

Susan No of course not—how could you? John did come with me but he's—Judy, I think I must be going out of my mind. I must be insane after all—I really must. There's no other possible explanation. (*She starts to cry*)

Judy Susan, please—just calm down and tell me what's happened. John's not left you, has he? You've not had a row, have you?

Susan Oh, no—nothing like that—nothing like that.

Judy What then?

Susan I've just told you, I don't know where to start.

Judy They do say that the beginning's a good place.

Susan Very well, I'll try. We came over on the ferry yesterday to Cherbourg. We drove down as far as Limoges—that is to say, John drove. He refused to let me do any of the driving. Anyway, we stopped at a hotel in Limoges and then, this morning, we did some shopping and drove down here the rest of the way. Oh, we stopped on the way and had some lunch.

Judy What time did you get here?

Susan About five, I think. Yes, it was—the clock was striking when we came into the house, I remember.

Judy Was there anyone here at the time?

Susan No, we went round to the keyholders to collect the keys. They're local people called Duval. They weren't in but they'd left the keys. So we came straight round here and opened up the house. Everything was fine. John was a bit tired after the drive but, otherwise, everything was great. Then John discovered he'd left his passport at the hotel in Limoges. At least he thought he had. He was in a bit of a state about it. He was just on the point of going out to the *tabac* to ring the hotel when this woman turned up.

Judy Woman? What woman?

Susan She said she was the owner.

Judy Of this place, do you mean?

Susan That's right.

Judy And was she?

Susan Yes. She said that the agents had let the place a week earlier than

Act II   21

she'd expected and she'd flown over to Bordeaux to check that everything was all right.

Judy I see. Well, that seems perfectly reasonable. What's wrong with that?

Susan Nothing, I suppose, except that she said she'd never let the house in May before. But she had—I know she had. We came here in May last year. I'm certain of that. It was the week after Father died. That was May seventeenth wasn't it?

Judy That's right—May seventeenth. You came to Bordeaux to see me. It must have been about a week after I'd got back from the funeral. I know it was May because I went on holiday to Corsica myself at the beginning of June.

Susan Then I must have been right.

Judy What did John say?

Susan That's the part I don't understand. He knows as well as I do when Father died but he made some remark about me getting muddled again. He must know, mustn't he?

Judy I would have thought so—yes. What did you say?

Susan I didn't want to argue in front of this woman so I said nothing more about it at the time. Anyway, to tell the truth, I began to wonder if I was getting confused again—you know, after what happened.

Judy Your illness, you mean?

Susan Exactly. I still get things mixed up sometimes. John's always on to me about it. Sometimes I'm positive that I'm right but he's so adamant I begin to have doubts. I mix up people and places—well, that's what John says, anyway.

Judy You make him sound like that character out of that play—what was it? *Gaslight*—that's right. You make sure he hasn't murdered an old woman up in the attic.

Susan We haven't got an attic.

Judy I know you haven't. It was meant to be a joke.

Susan Sorry, Judy—I wasn't thinking.

Judy Well, go on—what happened next?

Susan We had a few drinks and then this woman, April March she said her name was—

Judy April March?

Susan She said we weren't to laugh or anything.

Judy I'm not surprised—April March!

Susan Anyway, she said she was out of cigarettes and John said he was going up the road anyway to phone the hotel about his passport and he'd buy some for her at the *tabac*. So, he got in the car and drove off. And then . . .

Judy Yes?

Susan After he'd gone, I had a row with this April woman.

Judy A row? What about?

Susan It was all so ridiculous. I realize that now but, at the time, I just saw red and let her have it. It was quite stupid. I shouldn't have done it, I know, but it was almost as though she was deliberately trying to provoke me. I just had that feeling. I really don't know why.

Judy What did you say to her?

Susan I honestly can't remember, except that it was something to do with that awful cat.

Judy Cat? What cat?

Susan It's a ghastly stuffed black thing. It was sitting over there on the mantelpiece when we arrived. It's always there every year. I made John put it in that cupboard over there. Anyway, then I had this row. I think it was the cat that started it. I just can't remember. I have a vague recollection of getting it out of the cupboard and throwing it at her. At least, I think I did. Then I believe I told her to take the cat and get to hell out of here—or words to the effect.

Judy I see. Have you no idea why you did it?

Susan Not really—it's all confused in my mind.

Judy Did she go when you told her to?

Susan No. She said something about not letting us stay in this house again and then the front door opened and this man came in.

Judy Man? What man?

Susan The one I told you about, of course.

Judy Susan, you have said absolutely nothing about a man so far.

Susan I was sure I had.

Judy It doesn't matter. Go on.

Susan He just strolled in here as if he lived here, asked what all the row was about and then said he'd left his wallet on the table.

Judy Susan, I don't understand what you're saying.

Susan It can't have happened—it just can't. (*She rises and moves* DL)

Judy Susan, will you please explain—who was this man?

Susan Will you promise not to laugh at me?

Judy Of course I won't laugh at you.

Susan He said— (*she turns to face Judy*)—he said he was John.

Judy He said what?

Susan That he was John—my husband. He said he'd come back for his wallet.

Judy I don't believe it.

Susan I knew you wouldn't. It was a waste of time telling you. (*She turns away*)

Judy No—wait. (*She rises and moves towards Susan*) Do you promise me you're not making all this up?

Susan (*turning to Judy*) It's true. I know it's nonsense, but it's true. I swear it is.

Judy All right, then—I believe you. Now, what about the woman? What did she say when this man walked in and claimed to be your husband?

Susan That's the awful part. She just spoke to him as though he was John. She didn't turn a hair.

Judy And what did you say?

Susan Oh, Judy, I just lost control of myself. I just screamed and screamed and then everything started to spin round and round and then, I suppose, I must have fainted. I imagine they must have carried me in and put me on the bed in there. I don't remember anything at all about it.

Act II

Judy How long were you in the bedroom for?

Susan I've simply no idea. When I woke up, there was no sign of either of them. They'd just disappeared into thin air.

Judy Perhaps they were in the garden. Did you look out there?

Susan I searched everywhere for them—all over the house and round the garden. I went down the lane as far as the wood—there was no sign of them. Then I realized that both the cars had gone. That was the final straw. I just panicked. I ran up the lane and on to the main road to the *tabac* and phoned you. I didn't know what else to do. I was desperate.

Judy (*moving to the table and picking up the brandy bottle*) I think we could both use a drink. Where are the glasses?

Susan On the dresser. I'll get them.

Judy You sit down. I can find them.

Susan (*sitting down*) Thank you. It's very good of you, Judy—coming all this way.

Judy (*taking glasses from the dresser*) It's the very least I could have done when my big sister called for help, wasn't it? I'm sure you'd have done just the same if I'd have been the one in trouble. (*She pours out two drinks and hands one to Susan*) Here—get that down you. I'd say you need it. I most certainly do. (*She sits down*)

Susan Thank you. (*She drinks*) Judy, do you think I'm having hallucinations again?

Pause

Do you? Go on, don't be afraid to tell me what you think.

Judy I don't know what to say, Susan. I honestly don't. It all sounds so incredible—you must admit that. It sounds like something out of a Hitchcock movie. I ask you—a man comes in here, as cool as a cucumber and pretends to be your husband and then that woman with an impossible name—April March or whatever—agrees with him. It does take a bit of swallowing, you must admit.

Susan I knew that's what you'd say. I'd have taken a bet on it. I don't know why I bothered to tell you. I might just as well have saved my breath.

Judy Now, hold on a minute, Susan—hold on. All I'm trying to do is to be sensible about it.

Susan Whereas I'm not—is that what you're implying? Go on—say it. Is it?

Judy Now I don't think you're being exactly fair, are you, Susan? I didn't suggest you weren't being sensible, did I?

Susan Didn't you? It seemed very much like it to me. If that wasn't what you were suggesting, what did you mean?

Judy All I meant was that, on the face of it, it all seems a bit far-fetched—well, not far-fetched perhaps but, well—shall we say it takes a lot of believing. I think we ought to try and talk it over calmly and see if we can't come up with some sort of rational explanation.

Susan I see. I'm sorry, Judy. You are right, of course. But just tell me one thing—if it was some sort of hallucination, where's John now? Where has he gone? He's been away for hours.

Judy You have a point there, I'll admit. It's something I don't understand. The whole situation is so bizarre—uncanny almost.
Susan (*suddenly*) Judy, look—the bottle, the bottle of brandy. (*She rises*)
Judy What about it? It seems very good to me.
Susan No, no—I don't mean that. (*She picks up the bottle*) How many glasses do you think have been poured out of this bottle?
Judy I don't follow. What are you getting at?
Susan Judy, please—it's important.
Judy Well— (*taking the bottle*) —hardly any, I'd say, apart from our two glasses.
Susan Pour yours back into the bottle.
Judy Whatever for?
Susan Go on, please.
Judy I—oh, very well. (*She pours her drink back into the bottle*) I really don't see what you're getting at.
Susan (*excitedly*) Now mine—pour mine back as well.
Judy All right—if you say so. (*She pours Susan's drink back into the bottle*) There—now what?
Susan Don't you see?
Judy See what?
Susan Just as I thought. Now you've tipped our drinks back into it, the bottle is more than three-quarters full.
Judy Well?
Susan When that woman was here, we had at least three drinks each, out of that bottle—large ones too. That's nine glasses of brandy and look at it now—it's almost full.
Judy But you can't have done. It must be a different bottle.
Susan It isn't. It can't be. We only bought one bottle of brandy and one bottle of whisky on the boat coming over. We didn't open it until this evening.
Judy Perhaps it was the whisky you drank. You might have been mistaken.
Susan No—I'm positive it was brandy. I remember that woman saying that brandy was her favourite drink. (*She goes to the dresser*) Yes—look! (*She holds up the whisky bottle*) Here's the whisky. The seal's still intact. It's not been opened. (*She puts down the whisky and goes back to the table*) Don't you see?
Judy Frankly—no.
Susan Someone must have topped it up from another bottle and washed up the third glass. The other two we used were these here on the table. I know that one was mine—it's the only glass in the house with red grapes painted on it. I'm not certain about the other one.
Judy But why should anyone want to top the bottle up? I don't see the point.
Susan Neither do I—unless—unless . . .
Judy Unless what?
Susan Supposing that somebody wanted it to look as though there had been only two people here—John and me?
Judy And why on earth should anyone want that?

Act II 25

Susan I don't know. I don't know. (*She moves towards the fireplace*)
Judy There has to be some very simple solution. There just has to be.
Susan But what, for God's sake, what?
Judy Now, Susan, you'll have to forgive me for asking this. Please understand that I'm only trying to help, trying to be sensible. Is there any possibility that you were mistaken? You said, just now, that John reckons you mix things up. Do you think it could all have been a dream?
Susan (*turning*) Oh, yes—here we go again! I wondered how long it would be before we came round to that. I imagine these things, don't I? As long as I live, you'll go on thinking that, won't you? You'll be watching me—all of you—watching me to see if I do or say anything even the slightest out of the ordinary, won't you? Poor thing, you'll say, she had a breakdown, you know—never really got over it—never really recovered —still a bit mentally disturbed, you know. You musn't mind her. She's really quite harmless—just mad, that's all—just mad. Mad! Mad! Mad!
Judy (*rising*) Susan, pull yourself together, for God's sake.
Susan (*facing away from Judy*) Why should I pull myself together, as you put it? Why should I? (*Turning to face Judy*) Why should you want me to anyway—you of all people? I'd have thought it was in your interest for me to be insane. That's the only way you're going to get the—
Judy (*shouting*) Stop it, Susan! Stop it at once! Stop it, I say! (*She goes towards Susan*) That was a terrible thing to say, wasn't it?

Pause

Now, wasn't it?

Pause

It was, wasn't it? You know it was. I don't want anything of the kind. You must know that—surely you must. You are my sister. Your health and your happiness are more important to me than that—surely you must realize.

Judy leads Susan to the table

Now then.

Judy sits Susan down

Let's pour out those drinks again and talk it over and see what we can make of it, eh? (*She sits down*) That's sensible, isn't it?
Susan Yes, of course. I'm sorry, Judy. I'm sorry. I shouldn't have thought that of you. It's just that I've been rather edgy again lately. It's getting ready to go on holiday, I expect—I don't know. And now all this—I thought I was getting better. I really did.
Judy But you are—you are, Susan. You're so much better than when I came to stay with you in England; it's remarkable. You're like a different person.
Susan Yes—I know. Thank you, Judy. Thank you for answering my cry for help. I do appreciate it, I really do.

Judy (*squeezing her hand*) Fine! Fine! Now then, what about that drink? Or would you rather have a cup of coffee?

Susan Yes, coffee, please—I'd like that. Somehow, I don't want another drink out of that bottle. I know it's irrational but that's the way I feel about it.

Judy Right—coffee it is then. Where do you keep the saucepan? I'll get it. (*She rises*)

Susan It's in the cupboard under the dresser. I—Judy!

Judy What?

Susan I've just remembered something else. I used the saucepan to boil some water for coffee shortly after we arrived. I left it on the draining board over there. (*She rises*) It's gone—and the cups. They were on this table. We gave that woman a cup—I'm sure we did.

Judy Someone must have washed them up.

Susan But who?

Judy I've really no idea. Does it matter? Whoever it was saved you the trouble, didn't they? I'll get the saucepan. Where did you say it should be?

Susan In the bottom of the dresser if it's been put away. It's a small milk saucepan—a green one.

Judy (*moving to the dresser and sorting through the cupboard*) There's no saucepan like that here. There's a big one but no green one. Where else could it be?

Susan Perhaps whoever put it away didn't know where it went. They might have put it in that cupboard down there next to the sink—the one where I put the groceries.

Judy (*moving* DL) I'll look. (*She opens the cupboard* DL) Yes, there is a saucepan here. I don't know if it's the right one but it'll do anyway. Oh, my God!

Susan What is it, Judy? What is it?

Judy Nothing. (*She closes the cupboard door quickly*) Nothing at all. (*She stands in front of the cupboard door*)

Susan (*moving quickly* DL) I want to see. Show me what it is.

Judy Look, Susan—it's much better if you don't see. It'll only upset you again.

Susan Show me.

Judy Look, it isn't anything important. I promise you—really. It's just some stupid joke or the other.

Susan Let me see.

Judy Much better if you didn't—really.

Susan pushes Judy aside

Susan I must see, I must look. (*She kneels and opens the cupboard door and looks inside. She reaches in and then slowly pulls out the stuffed cat. It has no head and is covered with something that looks like blood*) Oh, my God! Oh, my God! Help me! Help me! (*She throws the cat on the floor and rises very slowly*) Oh, please—please—help me. (*The last is a long drawn out cry*)

Act II   27

Judy Look—it's someone playing a filthy joke—that's all. It's not a real cat after all, is it? There's no need to get so upset.
Susan It hasn't a head any more and it's covered with blood. Oh, Judy, Judy! (*She starts to cry*)
Judy Would you like to go and lie down for a while? I'll get rid of this thing and bring you in a cup of coffee, eh? Shall I do that?
Susan I don't know. I don't know what I want to do. Oh, Judy, I'm frightened.
Judy You go and lie down—you'll feel better after you've had a sleep. Will you do that, eh?
Susan All right—thank you, just for a few minutes. Get rid of it, Judy. You will get rid of it, won't you?
Judy I just said I would, didn't I?

Judy leads Susan towards the bedroom door

Susan Thank you, Judy—thank you. I'm sorry to be such a nuisance.
Judy You're not a nuisance at all. Think nothing of it. Get along now.
Susan Thank you.

Susan exits R

Judy goes to the window and takes a newspaper from the pile on the window-ledge. She returns DL, *spreads the paper on the floor, picks up the cat, wraps it in the newspaper and puts it on the table. She then opens the cupboard* DL, *takes out the saucepan, fills it with water, lights the gas and puts the water on to heat. She fetches two cups and saucers from the dresser and puts them on the table. She then picks up the bundle and exits* UL, *leaving the front door open*

After a moment, there is the sound of a car driving up and stopping, off. A car door slams

Susan enters R *and stands in the doorway*

Judy (*off*) Hello! Who's that? Oh, it's you. Wherever have you been. Susan's sick with worry. I think—
John (*off*) Judy! Whatever are you doing here?
Judy (*off*) Susan phoned me and asked me to come over.
Susan (*moving in to the room*) Is that you, John? Is that you?

John enters, followed by Judy

(*Rushing across to John*) John, where have you been? John, what's happened? I don't understand. I don't understand.
John What do you mean—"what's happened?" You know very well where I've been.
Susan I don't! I don't!
John But you do, for God's sake. Stop being so bloody childish. You're acting like an hysterical schoolgirl. I've been back to the hotel in Limoges to fetch my passport. You know very well I have. You offered to come with me, didn't you?

Susan No, John—you're wrong. I did nothing of the kind, you know I didn't.

John I say you did. I told you it would be better if you stayed here and you agreed. We opened the bottle of brandy and I had a quick glass before I went. When I left, you were sitting at this table drinking yours. Now, do you remember?

Susan How can I remember something which didn't happen? John, is this some kind of game you're playing? Nothing that you've just said is true. I know it isn't.

John Look, Susan, I've had about enough of your stupidity. I told you I'd be at least four hours. I rushed like the devil to get back here. (*He looks at his watch*) In fact, I've done it in slightly less than four hours. That'll give you some idea of the speed I've been driving at.

Susan He didn't say anything like that at all, Judy—honestly he didn't. I'm aware that I've been getting things a bit confused lately but this time I know I'm right. I'm absolutely certain of it.

John All right—calm down, Susan, please. We don't want one of your scenes. I suggest we all sit down and try and make some sense out of this. We can't both be right can we? What do you say?

Susan What earthly good will sitting down and talking do? You say you told me you were going back to the hotel and I know that you didn't. No amount of discussion is going to alter that.

John Please, Susan. We can't just leave it like that. It's an impossible situation, isn't it?

Susan Oh, very well—but on one condition.

John What's that?

Susan That you listen to what I have to say without dismissing it as nonsense.

John Right. I agree. Not that I . . .

Susan Not that you what?

John Never mind. Forget it. Come on, come and sit down. And you, Judy, please.

Susan All right. (*She sits down*)

John and Judy sit down, John next to Susan

This is ridiculous.

John In what way?

Susan You'd think we were going to hold an inquest. (*She starts to laugh*) I'm sorry, John it's all too absurd. It really is.

John (*starting to get up*) Very well—let's leave it, then if you're—

Susan Sit down, John, for Christ's sake. Let's get it over with.

John (*sitting*) O.K. O.K. But I'm bloody tired.

Susan Aren't we all? Judy's driven here from Bordeaux.

John So I gather. (*To Judy*) Why did Susan ask you to come here, Judy?

Judy She telephoned me. She was very upset, John. Quite honestly, I couldn't make much sense of what she was saying on the phone. Then the line went dead.

Act II 29

Susan That was all the money I had with me. I tried to get Judy back through the operator but there was some sort of mix-up.
Judy I waited for five minutes or so by the phone in case she rang again but when she didn't I decided to drive over and find out what it was all about.
John What started all this? How did you get into that state? You were fine when I left to get my passport.
Susan But you didn't say that was where you were going—you must know you didn't, John. We've been over all this already. You promised you'd listen to what I had to say. All you're doing is asking questions again.
John I'm sorry. You carry on then. What did you want to say?
Susan When you left here it wasn't to get your passport. You went to telephone the hotel from the box up the road and to get some cigarettes for that April March woman. And then you—
John What did you say? What woman?
Susan April March—you must remember.
John And who, in God's name, is April March?
Susan You know very well who she is. She's the woman who owns this place.
John I know nothing of the kind. Why should I go and get some cigarettes for the woman who owns this place?
Susan But you did, John. You know you did. She was here—in this room.
John What are you talking about? Susan, look, I can only suggest that you've been dreaming. Perhaps you feel asleep after I'd gone to Limoges and—
Susan (*rising*) I didn't dream it, I tell you. She was in this room. She sat at this table. Look, I'll describe her to you if you like—what she was wearing, what she looked like, the way she talked. She's an Australian, she said she came from—
John There was no woman here, I tell you, Australian, Russian, South African or any other bloody nationality.
Susan Look, John—look, please. We had three drinks each out of this bottle of brandy and then—
John (*picking up the bottle*) Out of this bottle? But it's—
Susan (*sitting down*) I know. I know—it just doesn't make any sort of sense.
John Exactly. (*He replaces the bottle*)
Susan She said she was out of cigarettes and you said you'd go to the *tabac* and get some for her. I know you did because you asked her if there was any particular brand she wanted and she said she preferred American. Now, I can't have dreamed that, can I, because I don't know the first thing about cigarettes.
John Susan, let's get this quite straight. I don't know any woman called April March or whatever you said. No woman of that name has ever been here—at least not while I've been in the house. I would hardly be likely to forget anyone with a name like that, would I?

Judy Look, John, the last thing I want to do is to interfere but Susan is pretty certain that woman did come here. She told me all about it. I'm quite convinced she's not imagining it, I honestly am.

John That's all very well, Judy, but how can she have been here? It just doesn't make any sort of sense.

Judy I don't know, John—I don't know. Anyway, that's not all of it by a long way. Tell him, Susan.

Susan What's the point of telling him the rest? He isn't going to believe that any more than he believes about Mrs March, is he?

John I'd like to believe you, I really would, but how can I when I know it isn't true? Anyway, this woman couldn't be the owner.

Susan Why not?

John Because the people who own this place are called Mercier. The Duvals told us last year. I remember it particularly because it's the same name as the champagne.

Susan But you said, this evening, that the owner lived in England.

John I said no such thing.

Susan Oh, God! There you go again. Why do you insist on denying everything you said? Mrs March said she bought the place from some local people. She didn't say when.

Judy That is a possibility, isn't it, John?

John If she'd been here, yes—but she wasn't here so it's all hypothetical, isn't it? No woman of that name came here this year, last year or any blasted year.

Susan In that case, why are you getting so het up about it?

John I'm not.

Susan Oh, but you are, John. Let me tell you, she knew all about this place. How do you explain that?

John She would do, wouldn't she? Oh, yes.

Susan I don't understand what you're getting at.

John If she was a figment of your imagination, she'd know as much as you know, wouldn't she?

Susan She knew about the Duvals. She knew about the *tabac* down the road and—wait, I've just thought of something.

John What?

Susan When she was telling us about getting food from the market in Ribérac, she said that market day was Thursday.

John I don't follow. What are you getting at?

Susan Thursday isn't market day in Ribérac. Friday is.

John So?

Susan If this April March is a figment of my imagination as you put it, then I would hardly be likely to imagine something which I knew to be wrong, would I?

Judy All this is getting us nowhere. Susan says the woman was here. You say she wasn't, John. As far as I can see, we're going to have to leave it at that.

Susan And the cat—what about that?

John Cat?

Act II

Susan You know very well which cat I mean. That horrid Satan that's always sitting on the mantelpiece when we get here.
John That! You surely remember. I put it away in that cupboard soon after we arrived, the same time as I put away those ornaments.
Susan It isn't in the cupboard now.
John It must be.
Susan All right, go and look then. It isn't there, I tell you.
John (*rising and going to the cupboard* DR *and opening it*) No, it isn't. Where the hell is it, then? (*He moves back to the table*)
Susan I can't tell you where it is.
John What do you mean—you can't tell me? Why not for God's sake?
Susan I want to tell you but I can't. It frightens me too much.
Judy Somebody cut its head off.
John They did what?
Judy They cut its head off and covered it with blood—or something that looks like blood anyway. I found it when I went to get the saucepan from the cupboard under the sink. I was going to make some coffee and I—Oh, Lord! I've left the saucepan on the stove. (*She rises and rushes over to turn off the gas*) It's all right. No harm done.
John You say you found it?
Judy Yes. Somehow, I have the feeling that I wasn't the one who was supposed to find it.
John What did you do with it?
Judy I wrapped it up in newspaper. I was going to take it and put it in that barn out there. In fact, I was on my way there when you turned up.
John Where is it now?
Judy I left it outside the front door. I would imagine it's still there. I doubt very much if it ran away.
Susan Don't, Judy—don't, please.
Judy Sorry—I forgot.
John Why the hell would anybody want to do a thing like that?
Judy I haven't the faintest idea.
Susan John, I'm frightened. I don't want to stay here tonight. I can't. I honestly can't.
John There is absolutely nothing to be frightened of—absolutely nothing at all. All you need is a good night's sleep and you'll have forgotten all about it in the morning. You take my word for it.
Judy You could both come and stay at my place if you like. I've only one spare room with a single bed but you're very welcome to use it.
Susan Could we, Judy? That would be marvellous. What do you say, John?
John Thank you, Judy—it's very kind of you to make the offer but I think we'll stay here. I see no point at all in Susan running away from these things. There is nothing to be scared of. If we came to your place she'd be giving in to this imaginary threat.
Susan Perhaps when you've heard the rest of the story you'll feel differently, John.
John The rest of the story?
Susan I haven't told you the worst part yet, John.

John If this is going to be another fairy story like April March, I suggest you make it a little more plausible.

Susan What's the use? You're making fun of me before I even start to tell you.

Judy (*moving to the table*) I think you'd better let her tell you, John.

John I'm not stopping her. (*He sits down*) What is it, Susan?

Judy sits down

Susan When you went out to get the cigarettes from—

John But I didn't. How can what you are going to tell me have any credibility if it's based on—

Susan John! Listen to me, please!

John All right. Go on.

Susan When you went out to get the cigarettes—or, at least, I think you went out—I was left on my own with Mrs March. After you'd gone we—well, we had a row. It was my fault I know. She was asking me about the time I was in hospital and I over-reacted. It ended up with her saying that she wouldn't allow us to stay in this house again. She was just about to go when—when . . .

John Yes?

Susan It's no use. You're not going to believe me.

John For God's sake, Susan, if you want to tell me, tell me. Stop acting like a five year old.

Susan Sorry. Well—the door opened and this man came in.

John What man?

Susan I don't know who he was. I've never seen him before in all my life. He said something about leaving his wallet on the table. I asked him who he was and—oh, God, he said he was my husband.

John Are you trying to tell me that this man, who you'd never seen before, came in here and said he was me?

Susan Yes, John.

John (*laughing*) Come off it, Susan. That's going too far even for you. Don't be so absurd. How could anybody possibly say they were me?

Susan But this man did, I tell you.

John What did he look like? Did he look like me?

Susan He was about your build—about your age, I'd say. He was even dressed like you. But it wasn't you—he didn't look like you at all. It wasn't you—it wasn't.

John You don't have to try to convince me. Whoever it was you dreamed up, it wasn't me.

Susan And then Mrs March just stood there and talked to him as though he really was you.

John But that's impossible.

Susan It was just a waste of time telling you. I knew it would be.

John Very well, go on then—what did you say to this man who said he was me?

Susan I didn't say anything. I just screamed. Then I must have passed out. When I came to it was much later. I was on the bed in there.

Act II   33

John That figures.

Susan What do you mean?

John It's exactly what I said. You went to lie down after I'd gone to get the passport. You fell asleep and dreamed it all—the woman who said she owned the place, the man pretending to be me and so on. When you woke up, you panicked and rang Judy. Don't you see, that has to be the explanation? Any other is so way out as to be nonsense. Don't you agree?

Susan No, I don't agree. I'm certain it all happened.

John What I don't understand is why you rang Judy. Why didn't you go round to the Duvals—they're only just round the corner?

Susan I thought they might still be out. Anyhow, I knew they wouldn't believe me—how could they?

John Quite. It's simply a matter of—

Susan Wait! I've just thought of something. When that man came in and said he was you, he said he'd forgotten his wallet. I remember now I looked at the table and your travel wallet was there, where I'd left it when I looked for your passport. How did he know the wallet was there?

John But it can't have been here. I took it with me when I went to Limoges. It's in the car now. I came in here in such a rush when Judy called me that I forgot to bring it in with me.

Susan It was here, John. I saw it. I know it doesn't make any sort of sense. I do see that. But what about the cat? Who took it out of the cupboard? If, as you say, there was nobody here after you left, who took it out of the cupboard and who did that to it? Who put it in that cupboard over there?

John I really have no idea—unless, of course . . .

Susan Unless I did it. That's what you are trying to say, isn't it?

John I didn't say so.

Susan But you're thinking it, though, aren't you? It's a nice tidy solution, isn't it? It has to be me, doesn't it?

Pause

Well, why don't you say it? (*Rising*) Go on, say it! Say it!

John (*rising*) I'm sorry, Judy. I think it's time Susan went to bed. It's been a long, tiring day for all of us. We could all do with some sleep. I'm not trying to rush you. There's a spare bed. You can stay the night if you like and save that drive back to Bordeaux.

Judy (*rising*) It's all right, John. It won't take long to get back. I'd rather, if you don't mind.

John That's entirely up to you. As I said, it's no trouble to us.

Judy Thanks, John—I'll get off. I'll come over again tomorrow if you want me to. Do you know my phone number?

John Susan does.

Judy Of course. Just give me a ring then, if you need me. I'd like to know how Susan is, anyway.

John Right. I'll do that.

Susan (*suddenly*) For Christ's sake!

John What is it?
Susan Stop talking as though I was some mentally deranged child. I don't care what you say, either of you. It all happened exactly as I told you. Why don't you believe me? Oh, dear God, why don't you believe me?

John leads Susan towards the door DR

John Come on, Susan love, come on—calm down and get off to bed. I'll bring you a drink as soon as Judy's gone. We'll talk about it again in the morning, if you want to. I'm so tired I can't think straight any more.
Susan (*starting to cry*) You believe me, don't you, Judy? Say you do, please.
Judy All right, Susan, there's no need to cry. I believe you. Now, you get off to bed and have a good sleep. Would you like me to stay with you for a while?
Susan No, thank you, Judy. I'll be all right. I will—honestly. You get off now. You've a long way to go and it's getting late. Good-night, Judy. Thank you again for coming over.
Judy Good-night. Sleep well.

Susan exits R

John closes the door after her and moves to the table

John (*quietly*) Well, what do you think?
Judy What do I think? I think she's going to pieces, I really do. She's talking and behaving like a child. I'd say it only needs to go on like this for a little longer and she'll be in that mental hospital again—and not just for a few weeks this time.
John Yes, that's how I see the situation too. I don't reckon she's far from the edge. One push and she'd be over. Come on, I'll see you to your car.
Judy Right. (*She moves to the door* UL *and checks*) I've just remembered the cat.
John What about it?
Judy It's still in the newspaper outside the front door. Would you like me to take it with me and dump it somewhere?
John No—leave it where it is. I'll see to it later.
Judy Right. John, you'll treat her gently, won't you?
John (*moving up to Judy*) Don't worry, Judy. I know what I'm doing. You'd better be off now.
Judy Right.

Judy exits UL, *followed by John*

(*Off*) Let me know if you need me for anything.
John (*off*) Will do. See you, Judy.
Judy (*off*) See you, John.

There is the sound of a car starting up and driving off

Act II

After a few seconds, the Man enters UL *carrying the newspaper bundle which he puts on the cupboard* DL. *He goes to the table, picks up the brandy bottle and takes it to the dresser. He takes the whisky bottle and a glass and returns to the table. He pours himself a large whisky which he drinks in one go. He then pours out a second. He takes the glass to the front door* UL *and bolts it. He then crosses to the door* R

Man (*calling*) I'm bringing you your drink, Susan. Judy's gone. I've locked up. We're all on our own now.

He opens the door, turns off the living-room light from the second switch by the door and exits R *into the bedroom, closing the door after him*

The stage is in darkness as—

the CURTAIN *falls*

ACT III

The same. The next morning, about 8.30 am

When the CURTAIN *rises, the room is bathed in sunlight. The Man is seated at the table eating a breakfast of bread, butter and coffee. He is listening to the radio. After a moment or two, there is a knock at the door* UL. *He turns off the radio*

Man (*calling*) Who is it?
Mrs March (*off*) It's me. Let me in.
Man (*calling*) Coming. (*He rises*) Won't be a tick. (*He goes to the door* UL *and unbolts it*)
Mrs March (*off*) Is it all right to come in?
Man Yes. I'm on my own. Nobody else is here.

Mrs March enters

(*Closing the door*) Would you like some coffee? I've just made some.
Mrs March Good idea.
Man The cups are on the dresser behind you. (*He sits down*)
Mrs March Oh, right. (*She takes a cup and saucer from the dresser and sits down*)
Man (*pushing over the coffee-pot*) Help yourself.
Mrs March (*coldly*) Thank you. (*She pours her coffee*)

Pause

Well, come on—are you going to sit there all morning without uttering a sound?
Man I'm having my breakfast.
Mrs March So I've noticed.
Man I've earned it.
Mrs March I'm glad to hear it.

Pause

Well, I'm waiting to hear how it went.
Man Exactly to plan.
Mrs March It did?
Man Like bloody clockwork.
Mrs March Beauty!
Man Yes. (*He pauses*) Look, I don't like it. I don't like it at all.
Mrs March I thought you just said it went according to plan.
Man It did. All the same, if you'd told me the details beforehand, I don't think I'd have touched this one.

Act III

Mrs March Why not, for God's sake?

Man When you told me what I had to do, it all seemed different somehow. It was some woman I didn't know—a stranger. It's quite another kettle of fish when you see the person, isn't it?

Mrs March What do you mean? I don't understand what you're getting at.

Man Perhaps you would if you'd been here last night when I walked into that room. I'm telling you, as long as I live I'll never be able to forget the look on her face when she looked up and saw who it was. It was sheer bloody terror.

Mrs March That was what was supposed to happen, wasn't it?

Man I know that. There didn't seem anything to it when we talked about it beforehand but last night . . .

Mrs March Are you getting cold feet or something?

Man No.

Mrs March What then?

Man I don't know—it's just that she seems such a nice, harmless woman.

Mrs March That really is quite beside the point.

Man I'm not at all sure that I'm going to be able to see it through.

Mrs March There's nothing more to see through. He said he'd be back here at nine o'clock. (*She looks at her watch*) It's quarter to now. All you have to do now is to change places with him, when he gets here, and then we both disappear—after he's paid us the money. We'll be back in England by tonight and, as far as we are concerned, it's over and done with. We've played our parts. The next stage is up to him. That's right isn't it?

Man I suppose so. I don't see why I had to come back to this place at all. After I'd left her in the hospital, why couldn't we have both shoved off?

Mrs March Not on your life. Supposing somebody from the hospital had come round here in the night with a message or something. That would have been marvellous, wouldn't it? Disappearance of husband after taking his wife into hospital.

Man Look, don't you think it's time I was told what all this is about?

Mrs March You will be.

Man I think I should have been told in the first place. How the hell can I be expected to do the job properly if I'm left in the dark like this?

Mrs March Stop whinging, Andy. You know very well that was part of the agreement between John and me. I was the only one, apart from him, to know the complete plan. The arrangement was that you were to carry out what you were told to do as the situations arose.

Man Well, I think it was a bloody stupid way of carrying on. Didn't he trust me or something?

Mrs March He didn't know you, did he? I gave him my assurance that you were reliable and could be counted on to carry out a job discreetly. He took my word for it.

Man Why should he take your word? He didn't know you all that well, did he?

Mrs March John and I had met several times during the past few weeks when he was working it all out. We came to know each other quite well.

Man (*rising*) I bet you bloody did. I know you of old. I notice it's John this and John that. I suppose he's been screwing you, has he?
Mrs March Stop talking nonsense.
Man Has he?
Mrs March Has he what, for God's sake?
Man Been screwing you.
Mrs March I said—"stop talking nonsense."
Man I'm not so sure it is nonsense. I wouldn't be at all surprised if there's a lot more to this whole business than I know about—not that I know a fat lot now. (*He goes up to the window and looks out*)
Mrs March Look, Andy, I know how you must feel about being kept in the dark like this but it wasn't my idea—honestly it wasn't. He insisted we played it that way. He said I wasn't to tell you the details until we'd pulled it off. So, just be patient for a bit longer and then I'll tell you. You have my word—all right?
Man (*turning to face Mrs March*) I haven't much option, have I?
Mrs March First of all, I must know exactly what happened last night.
Man (*sitting down*) O.K. Right—what do you want to know?
Mrs March You took the drink in to her, did you?
Man Yes, God! It was awful. She looked up and saw me, standing there in the doorway. To begin with, I think she thought it was her husband. Then, gradually, I saw the truth dawning on her. I don't think I've ever seen anyone so frightened before—ever. Then she let out this God-awful scream. She just sat there in her bed and screamed and screamed.
Mrs March All right—all right. I get the picture loud and clear. Now get on with it. What did you do then?
Man I put the drink down on the bedside table and walked out of the room. I came in here and fetched that bloody cat out of the parcel. Then I got its head from where we'd hidden it behind the stove and pinned it back on again like you told me to. I didn't make a very good job of it. In fact, it looked pretty revolting. Anyway, I unbolted the front door and went round the back of the house. He'd left the shutters of the bedroom window unlatched, as he said he would. I pulled them open slightly and propped the blasted cat on the outside ledge.
Mrs March She didn't see you?
Man No, the bed has its back to the window. Then I returned to the house and went through that door. She'd calmed down a bit by then—well, she'd stopped screaming anyway. But when she saw me standing there, she started all over again. I tell you, I very nearly jacked it in there and then. I felt as though—
Mrs March Never mind how you felt. What did you do then?
Man I told her to pull herself together or something like that and then I said I'd open the window to give her some air. Then I pretended that the window was stuck and that I couldn't open it. She turned round to face the window. I moved on to one side so that she could have a clear view. The moon had just come up and there was that repulsive cat sitting on the other side of the window bathed in moonlight. Her husband was dead right. He must have known exactly how she'd react.

Act III

You told me she was scared of cats. You weren't joking. It worked like bloody magic. I wouldn't have believed it unless I'd seen it for myself. She just went out of her mind. She was like a gibbering maniac.

Mrs March And then?

Man I did exactly what you'd told me to do. I moved the key of that door to this side and locked it and left her in there looking at that thing. Then I went up to the phone box and rang the hospital. I had a bit of a job making them understand. You know my French isn't too hot. I think they were telling me to take her to her doctor but, in the end, I got them to understand that we didn't live round these parts and they agreed that I could take her to the hospital. They told me to get an ambulance. You didn't tell me I'd have to do that. I thought they'd send one for her. Anyway they gave me a number to ring and I got one almost straight away. I came back here, sneaked round the back and managed to remove the cat without her seeing me and then came in here and waited for the ambulance. I didn't go back into her bedroom but I could hear her through the door. She was still carrying on. Then the ambulance turned up. It was quite amazing the speed the men worked at. They had her into the ambulance in next to no time. She's calmed down quite a bit. I think they must have given her a jab or something.

Mrs March What happened when you arrived at the hospital?

Man They carted her off straight away. Then, after I'd paid off the ambulance, I went to see the man who was in charge and they started asking me a lot of questions.

Mrs March What did you tell them?

Man I was a bit worried to begin with because, let's face it, I didn't know much about her past history. So I pretended not to understand what they were saying. There wasn't anyone on duty who could speak English so it worked out O.K.

Mrs March John knew there wouldn't be. He'd made discreet enquiries.

Man They suggested I left her there and came back in the morning when there'd be someone on duty who could understand English.

Mrs March Did they say what they were going to do?

Man Not exactly. They said something about getting in touch with her doctor in England. Fortunately, you'd told me the name of the hospital she'd been in before so I was able to tell them that. Well, that was it, really, as far as last night went. They rang up for a taxi for me at the hospital and I came back here. I went into the other bedroom and had a sort of sleep until about seven or so.

Mrs March You didn't get in touch with John, did you?

Man Of course not. You'd told me not to. Not that I knew where he was anyway.

Mrs March You weren't suppose to know.

Man No. All I knew was that you'd said he'd be here at nine o'clock this morning and take over from me providing everything had worked out as planned.

Mrs March Well, it certainly seems to have done. (*She rises and moves to the fireplace*)

Man There's something I don't understand—not that I understand any bloody thing if it comes to that.

Mrs March (*turning to the Man*) What don't you understand.?

Man What happens when he goes to see her at the hospital today? Surely they'll realize it's not the same man.

Mrs March It is a slight risk, yes, but it was one we were prepared to take. You don't have to worry about it. We've been gambling on two things. Firstly, it was the night staff on duty when you took her in. I doubt very much if any of them will be there this morning. Secondly, you're both about the same build. You both speak poor French. They were far more concerned about her than they were about you. I don't imagine for one moment they'll even begin to suspect you're not the same person. After all, why should they?

Man Let's hope you're right.

Mrs March The whole thing was very much of a gamble. As it happens, it's worked very much sooner than either of us thought it would. It could have taken days, weeks even, to get her into that hospital. It might not have worked at all. There was always that possibility.

Man A fairly remote one, I'd say. He must have been pretty certain it was going to work or he wouldn't have gone off and arranged to meet us here this morning.

Mrs March In fact, this was only plan number one. If that had failed, we had other ideas.

Man But supposing it had failed. All I was told was that if she didn't react sufficiently to the cat business, I was to lock her in the bedroom and beat it. Would he have left her there until nine o'clock this morning?

Mrs March I've just told you—we had other plans for that eventuality.

Man What were they?

Mrs March It doesn't matter now, does it?

Man (*rising and moving* DL *slightly*) Well, I'll tell you something. If it hadn't come off last night, you could have counted me out from now on.

Mrs March Well, it did come off—so that's purely academic, isn't it? There's nothing more for you to do now apart from picking up your share of the proceeds. Or are you planning to refuse it on moral grounds?

Man (*turning to face Mrs March*) On the contrary. I don't think it's enough—not for what we've done. I think it's worth a bloody sight more than three thousand.

Mrs March Hard luck! Three thousand's what we agreed with him and that's all we're going to get.

Man I've only your word for it that he's paying three thousand. How do I know he isn't paying you a bloody sight more than that?

Mrs March You don't, do you? You'd better ask him when he gets here.

Man Even if three's what you agreed, I don't think it's enough.

Mrs March What are you getting at?

Man That's my business. Let's call it a little secret from you. That makes a change, doesn't it?

Mrs March (*moving towards the Man*) Look, If you've got any mad

Act III 41

ideas about blackmail, I'd forget them if I was you. It's not exactly in your line, anyway, is it?
Man It might be worth the risk. I'll try anything once.
Mrs March Forget it. Forget it, do you hear me? I'm up to my neck in this as well, remember—more so in fact. All you had to do was what you were told to do.
Man We've always worked as a team before—you and me. It was different this time. I don't think I like it. In fact, I'm bloody well sure I don't. It smells. (*He moves* DL)
Mrs March In what way were things different this time?
Man (*turning to her*) Well, they were, weren't they? We've been in the con-game for a long time you and me. We've always made a good living out of it, haven't we? And we've never been caught—not once. We've always had the good sense to move on when we've worked the district for a while.
Mrs March I don't see what you're getting at.
Man I'll tell you what I'm getting at. Up till now it's only been a matter of separating bloody fools from their money. Oh, I'm sure they were upset at the time—hard up in some cases, I don't doubt—but they recovered after a bit. There was no real harm done—no permanent damage. But, this time, we've been responsible for putting an innocent woman into a mental hospital—helped to push her over the edge so that some bloke we don't even know can get her certified. I don't even understand why he wants her put away. I don't like it, I tell you. I don't like it at all.
Mrs March Christ, you are in a state, aren't you? Look, when he turns up, you'd better let me do all the talking.
Man Please yourself—suits me. I'm out of my depth. I don't mind admitting it. Answer me one thing—that's all. Why the hell did he want her put away?
Mrs March I'll tell you later. I'll tell you when we get away from here.
Man No—that won't do. I want to bloody well know now.
Mrs March Why, for God's sake? Why is it so important for you to know right now?
Man I have my reasons.
Mrs March What reasons?
Man That's my business. Why should I tell you? You've told me sod all.
Mrs March Is it something to do with blackmail?
Man No—nothing like that. I swear to God it isn't.
Mrs March All right then. Just stop whinging and I'll tell you. (*She sits down*)
Man That's more like it. (*He sits down*) Now then—tell me—why does he want her put into a mental home?
Mrs March I'm not absolutely sure.
Man Come off it.
Mrs March You have to believe me. I only know what he told me. I gather it's something to do with some large amount of money her father left her in his will. There was some sort of condition. It seems she wont'

come into the money for another three months anyway and then only if she's of sound mind—or whatever the legal jargon is.
Man You mean that if she's declared insane, then he comes into the money? Is that it?
Mrs March I suppose so. He didn't say. That must be it, mustn't it, otherwise he wouldn't have gone to all that trouble, would he?
Man He must be pretty certain or he wouldn't be prepared to fork out three thousand, would he? I'm surprised he can lay his hands on all that ready. What is he? Did he tell you?
Mrs March Works in a bank, I think. He didn't say which one.
Man In a bank, eh? Oh, yes. Perhaps he's helped himself to some of their lolly and he needs the inheritance to pay it back. How much does he stand to get from this little lark? Did he say?
Mrs March I've no idea. He didn't go into that. It must be a sizeable amount if he's prepared to shell out three thousand pounds on the chance of getting it.
Man Agreed. All the same, look at the risk we're taking. It's a bit different from conning some mug out of the odd fifty with a hard luck story, isn't it?
Mrs March I suppose so—yes.
Man There's no suppose about it. Talking of the odd fifty, I think we'd better start thinking about moving on again, don't you? I reckon we've cleaned up all that we're likely to get from that village. Some of the shopkeepers are starting to make noises about wanting their money and there are no more shops left in the area who'll give us credit. Might be a good thing to get away from there anyway. Where do you fancy?
Mrs March I'm not bothered—just as you like.
Man You don't sound very concerned. What is it? You haven't got other plans, have you?
Mrs March I might have and then, on the other hand, I might not.
Man My God, I believe you have. It's this bloody man, isn't it? (*He rises and moves in front of the table*)
Mrs March Suppose it is. I'm not under any contract to you, am I? We're not married, are we? I can live my own life if I want to, can't I?
Man You had all this worked out, didn't you? You just used me. That's why you left me in the dark about this job. You've got this sucker in tow, haven't you? I get half of a measly three thousand, and what do you get? You get half a bloody fortune don't you?
Mrs March (*rising*) Stop whinging, you bloody stupid bastard. You've got it all wrong. You're letting your imagination get the better of you. Now, calm down. Do you want him to find us at each other's throats when he arrives? Do you?
Man Well—no.
Mrs March Right then. Just take my word for it, this is a business deal between the two of us. It's always been that and it's going to stay that way. Convinced? Prepared to leave it at that?
Man Have I got any choice?

Act III

Mrs March Quite honestly—no, you haven't. (*She pauses*) Now, for Christ's sake, sit down and try and pull yourself together. He's due any minute.
Man Oh, all right. (*He sits*)
Mrs March (*sitting*) That's better.
Man (*after a pause*) How did you meet this bloke, then?
Mrs March Does it matter?
Man To me—yes. You said you'd tell me.
Mrs March I met him when I was working that hotel at Stratford. There was some sort of week-end conference being held there. He was sitting on his own in the bar. It seems that all the other delegates had gone to the theatre and he'd opted out. I wouldn't imagine Shakespeare was his scene particularly. Anyway, we struck up a conversation and—
Man You mean, you picked him up, don't you?
Mrs March Not exactly. I wouldn't say that. We had a drink or two, that's all. The next night, I saw him again and he asked me if I'd like to go out to dinner with him.
Man What about the conference? Didn't they have sessions in the evening?
Mrs March I don't know. He didn't seem to be tied up anyway. I said I wasn't doing anything important so I agreed to go with him. He took me to the *Hilton*.
Man *Hilton*, eh?
Mrs March Why not?
Man Nothing. Go on.
Mrs March While we were having dinner, he told me that the manager of the hotel where we were both staying had seen us in the bar the previous night. He mentioned it to John and said he had his doubts about me—thought I was working a racket or something. God knows who tipped him off. I thought I'd been careful. Then John asked me if there was anything in the manager's allegations and, of course, I denied it. He didn't seem very convinced and then I started to get worried. I thought he might be the law or something. Then he told me what it was all about. He suggested I might like to do a job for him.
Man What did you say to that?
Mrs March Well, there was still the chance he was the law or some private enquiry agent so I pretended not to know what he was on about. Then he asked me to think about it. Said he would make it worth my while and so on. He didn't mention it again all evening but he asked me to see him again the next night—that was Sunday.
Man And you saw him again?
Mrs March Yes. I said I'd been thinking over what he'd said the night before and that it was just possible that I might be interested.
Man And then he told you what he had in mind?
Mrs March Just a brief outline and what he was prepared to pay. To cut a long story short, I said I'd do it. I told him I had a friend who'd help me.
Man Me?
Mrs March Exactly. And that's it really. I've seen him several times since

then to work out the details. We had several other plans if this one had failed but, as it happens, they weren't needed.

Man I see. What I still don't understand is why it was necessary for you to come here and pretend to be the owner. What did that achieve?

Mrs March Well, first of all, if you were to be sufficiently frightening as her supposed husband when you switched with John last night, it was imperative that there was a third party here to corroborate your story. Secondly, if we were to convince her that she was going out of her mind, we had to invent at least two imaginary people who would disappear without trace when she tried to convince John otherwise. That's why we had to top up the brandy.

Man But there were so many things that could have gone wrong.

Mrs March You don't have to tell me. We were taking a hell of a lot of risks.

Man We nearly dropped a clanger over the money. You told me to remove all the small change from her handbag in case she rushed off to make a phone call after we'd left her. Then you go and leave five francs on the table for the cigarettes. It was a bloody good job I noticed it just as we were going out.

Mrs March Yes, Andy—so you told me at the time. Anyway, it didn't make any difference as it happens. She must have had a couple of francs in her pocket or something because she managed to make a phone call after all. That's how her sister came to be here.

Man I see. Anything else go wrong?

Mrs March I slipped up once or twice. I thought he'd filled me in pretty thoroughly with the details of the area around here but I mixed up the market days in the local town. I didn't notice it at the time but he did and he told me about it afterwards. Then there was the business of letting the place in May. When I was pretending to be the owner, I said I didn't let before the beginning of June and she insisted they'd been here last year in May. She was right, of course, but he covered it up in a sort of way. I don't think she was totally convinced but it didn't really matter as it happens. She thought she was getting things muddled again.

Man You were dead lucky there, if you ask me. It was a pretty narrow escape. Was that all?

Mrs March More or less. She did ask about a sort of transport café I hadn't heard of but I passed it off, I think.

Man The trickiest part for me was waiting outside after you'd gone in pretending to be the owner. When he came out on the pretext of going to the café, I only had a couple of minutes to take in all the details of what had happened since they arrived. It wasn't easy, believe me.

Mrs March I'm sure it wasn't. Mind you, getting that row going wasn't easy for me, either.

Man What row?

Mrs March That was part of the plan. I had to get her worked up so she'd be in a state of near hysteria when you arrived. You know—one thing on top of another. As it happened, she gave me a good lead. I was damn lucky.

Act III

Man As usual. (*He pauses*) Before that, when he was here, she didn't ask where you lived or anything, did she?

Mrs March As a matter of fact, she did.

Man What did you say?

Mrs March I told her I lived near Hythe.

Man What the hell did you say that for?

Mrs March It seemed sensible to me at the time to use a place where we'd lived once. I wouldn't be likely to slip up on details if she knew it, would I?

Man She didn't know it, I hope.

Mrs March Not very well, I don't think. She did say she'd been there for a short holiday once but that's all. She wouldn't have been likely to have known a Mr and Mrs March, would she?

Man No—I see what you mean. (*He laughs*) My God—April March! Wherever did you dream up a name like that from?

Mrs March I think it's a very good name.

Man I think it's bloody ridiculous.

Mrs March Exactly. It's so ridiculous that anyone would think it had to be authentic.

Man I suppose we'd better start thinking of new names if we're moving on to another hunting ground. God, I've had so many, I sometimes forget what my real name is.

Mrs March That's a fact.

Man (*looking at his watch*) He's late. What happens if he doesn't turn up? What do we do then? Have you thought of that?

Mrs March He will. Don't worry so much.

Man I wish we knew where to get in touch with him.

Mrs March Well, we don't, do we?

Man (*rising*) No. I don't, anyhow. Just a minute—if he told you about the mistakes you'd made last night, where did you see him if you don't know where he is?

Mrs March Up at the café after I'd left you here to make your second appearance—remember?

Man Remember? I'm not likely to forget, am I? I spent hours hiding behind that bloody barn.

Mrs March Well, it's all over, so stop moaning. We'll be collecting soon, don't forget.

Man Let's hope so. He's bloody late. (*He collects the dirty plate and cups etc. from the table*)

Mrs March What are you doing?

Man Just tidying up.

Mrs March Whatever for?

Man (*moving to the sink with the dirty crockery*) I'd rather wash them up and put them away. Better not to leave any evidence behind. You never know.

Mrs March Just as you please. (*She rises*) I'll give you a hand. Not that it matters. They're hardly likely to come and test the cups for fingerprints, are they?

Man (*turning to her*) The police, you mean? How could the police get involved in this?

Mrs March Calm down—no need to get the jitters. I was only joking. Why would the police suspect anything?

Man No, of course not. Stupid of me. You're right of course. (*He runs water into the bowl and starts to wash the dishes*)

Mrs March takes the tea-towel and dries the dishes as he passes them to her

Mrs March I usually am.

Man Yes. (*He pauses*) I've just thought of something else.

Mrs March What now?

Man What if the real owner had turned up? That would have put the kybosh on the whole thing, wouldn't it?

Mrs March No problem. He'd thought of that. He checked up with the agents. He told them some story about wanting to contact the owners for some reason or the other. He was in luck, as it happens. The owner had gone to Canada to visit his daughter.

Man And what about those locals you were telling me about—the keyholders, how did he get rid of them?

Mrs March He didn't. It just happened that way. It couldn't have worked out better.

Man You wouldn't believe it, would you? He's a right jammy bastard.

Mrs March (*moving up to the dresser with the crockery and putting it away*) I wish he'd hurry up. I'm starting to get a bit worried myself. The sooner we get away from this place the better, as far as I'm concerned.

There is the sound of a car driving up and stopping, off

Man That'll be him now. (*He dries his hands on the towel and puts it on the cupboard by the sink*)

The door opens and John enters UL

John Sorry I'm a bit late. I was held up behind some sort of cycle race. Well, how did it go?

Mrs March Fine. Just the way you reckoned it would. First time too.

John Where is she?

Man She's in the mental wing of the local hospital.

John She is? God, that's a relief. Well done, both of you. I didn't think we'd pull it off quite so soon. (*To the Man*) What are the arrangements?

Man I said I'd go back to the hospital this morning to talk it over with the doctor. There was only a male charge nurse on last night.

John That's what I gambled on. What did he say?

Man I pretended not to understand most of what he was saying.

John Good.

Man Not that I could anyway even if I'd wanted to. He said that there would be someone there this morning who could speak English.

John That's how I understood it would be. What time did you say I'd be there?

Man Ten o'clock. I hope that was O.K.

Act III

John Fine.
Man Well, it's over to you now.
John Quite. What sort of state was she in?
Man Terrible. I didn't like it at all, I don't mind telling you.
John What do you mean?
Man Well, if you ask me, it was bloody pathetic. I felt really sorry for her. God, you must hate her to do that to her.
John I'm not paying you to feel sorry or to give me your opinions. Understand?
Man I suppose so.
John You've done your part. It doesn't concern you any more.
Man I realize that but all the same—
John All the same nothing. (*He takes a packet from his inside pocket and throws it on the table*) I didn't know if it would work first time but I brought the money with me all the same. There's three thousand in used twenties there. That's what we agreed, wasn't it?
Mrs March That's right, John—three thousand in cash.
John You'd better count it to make sure I haven't short-changed you.
Mrs March No need for that. I trust you. You know that, don't you? I wouldn't be likely to—
Man It's not enough.
John (*turning on him*) What do you mean—not enough? I said three thousand and that was agreed by your—by your friend here.
Man But I didn't agree, did I? It was all fixed up between the two of you. It seems a piddling amount for all the risks we've taken.
John Well, that's all you're going to get. Take it or leave it.
Man I don't think you realize the situation somehow. We know all about this, don't we? We could make things very uncomfortable for you if we wanted to, couldn't we?
John You don't know anything about it at all. You're just bluffing.
Man Oh, but I do. I know all about it. Well, perhaps not all but enough to make things pretty hot for you if I felt that way.
John How do you know? (*To Mrs March*) Did you tell him? I thought I told you not to tell him the details.
Mrs March I didn't think it mattered—not now, not once we'd pulled it off.
John (*shouting*) I told you to keep your mouth shut. Why the hell did you have to blab it all out to him?
Mrs March I'm sorry, John. I really am. I honestly reckoned it didn't matter now, my word, I didn't. He won't say anything. I promise. I'll see he doesn't.
John Well, he'd better not. (*To the Man*) As for you, my friend, you just listen to me. That money on the table is all you're going to get from me—not a penny more. And if you've any bloody stupid ideas about blackmail you can forget them here and now. Understand?
Man So help me, did I say anything about blackmail? Did I?
John No—not exactly but you made your meaning reasonably clear all the same.

Man All I meant was that I thought it was worth more than three thousand. I still do.

Mrs March Drop it, Andy—drop it! Do you hear?

Man All right. I won't say another word but let me tell you here and now that if you two have any fancy ideas about—

John (*to Mrs March*) What's he on about?

Mrs March Oh, nothing—nothing at all really. Don't take any notice of him. He never did know when he was beaten.

John All right. Let's leave it at that then. (*He turns back to the Man*) Did you sign any papers or anything last night?

Man Of course not. What sort of fool do you take me for? I told them I'd see to all that this morning if it was necessary.

John Good. It all seems quite straightforward then. Well, I won't keep you any longer. I expect you're both anxious to get off.

Mrs March We're just going to fetch the case from the hotel and then we'll make our way back to Bordeaux for the plane.

John You're not both staying in the same hotel, are you?

Man You've got to be joking, mate. I'm not staying in any bloody hotel. I spent the night here—remember?

John Quite—yes, of course. Well now then—you'd better not both go off together.

Mrs March Don't worry, we won't. (*To the Man*) You take the car and drive up as far as the *tabac*. Wait for me there. I'll walk up and you can pick me up and drive into Ribérac. O.K.?

Pause

What's up?

Man Nothing. I'm just surprised I'm not the one who has to do the bloody walking, that's all. (*He moves to the door* UL) Right—I'm off. (*To John*) Cheerio, then.

John Aren't you going to take your money?

Man Christ!

John (*throwing the packet to him*) Here, catch. I'd put it away safely if I was you.

Man Don't worry, I will. (*To Mrs March*) Are you coming?

Mrs March In a minute. You carry on.

Man All right, but don't be long. (*He stays by the door*)

Mrs March (*to John*) Thank you. I enjoyed working with you.

John Enjoy is hardly the word I'd use, Christine. Nevertheless—

Man Come on, for God's sake.

John I'll see you out.

The Man, Mrs March and John exit UL. *There is the sound of a car starting up and driving off. John re-enters. He goes to the dresser and pours himself a large drink which he drinks standing by the dresser. He then goes to the door* UL *and calls*

O.K. You can come in now. (*He moves to the table*)

Judy enters and stands in the doorway

Act III

(*Moving towards her*) Did you hide the car? They didn't see you, did they?
Judy No—I parked it down the lane by the wood.
John Good. Oh, Judy!

She runs to him and he takes her in his arms and kisses her

(*Holding Judy at arm's length*) Judy darling, it's worked. It's worked.
Judy I just can't believe it. Where is she now?
John Exactly where I'd planned she'd be. If what that wretched man Hart—or whatever his real name is—says is true, she's really cracked up this time.
Judy What will you do?
John I'll get her transferred to that mental hospital in Cirencester where she was before. I doubt if there'll be any problem about that. They said if there was any serious reoccurrence they'd take out a section or whatever the jargon is. Then we're home and dry. Judy, my darling, you're going to be rich.
Judy And so are you.
John In a way, yes. But you're the one who'll inherit the money if she's certified insane, aren't you?
Judy That's nonsense. It will be our money—yours and mine. I always said it would be—didn't I?
John Bless you. Thank you, Judy.
Judy No need to thank me, John. You're the one who planned it all. You and that dreadful woman. (*She moves away slightly*) John, there's something I want to ask you. (*Turning to him*) Would you tell me the truth?
John What do you want to ask?
Judy That woman—did you lead her to believe that there would be more in it for her than the three thousand pounds? (*She pauses*) Did you, John?
John I don't understand.
Judy I think you do, John. You didn't tell her about us, did you?
John Of course I didn't. That would hardly have been wise, would it?
Judy No, it wouldn't. Did you give her the idea that she might be sharing the inheritance with you? Did you?
John What a preposterous idea.
Judy Did you, John?
John Good God—no. No really, I swear it, Judy—believe me.
Judy (*laughing*) "The lady doth protest too much, methinks."
John I don't follow. What lady? What are you on about?
Judy Forget it. It doesn't matter.
John But I want to know what you meant.
Judy I said forget it, John. I intend to. (*She pauses*) Well, we've pulled it off—that's the main thing. There were some very uncomfortable moments though. I was shattered when she phoned me last night.
John I don't know where she got the money from for the call. I'd instructed that man to take all the coins out of her purse.
Judy When she phoned, I thought something must have gone wrong.

That's why I drove over. I knew you'd said to keep away until it was all over but I felt it would be wiser for me to come under the circumstances.

John I'm glad you did.

Judy And that horrid cat. I had no idea it was in that cupboard. It nearly finished me when I found it there. No wonder it had the effect on her that it did.

John Poor Judy. How do you think I felt when she turned up at the *tabac* to make the phone call? That's where I was when I was supposed to have gone into Limoges for my passport. I was in the bar.

Judy On your own?

John Of course, why?

Judy I just wondered if that woman was with you.

John No. She had been, earlier on, but she'd left by the time Susan arrived. She'd only called in for a minute to let me know how things had gone. That was part of the arrangement.

Judy I see.

John I was scared stiff that Susan might come into the bar to ask for some change or something.

Judy You don't think she suspects anything, do you?

John About us, do you mean?

Judy Yes.

John No. She hasn't the faintest idea. I'm positive of that.

Judy (*sitting on the edge of the table*) I just wondered if she found it strange —all those business trips you've made to the Continent recently.

John Oh, I don't think so—not for one minute. The business trips were genuine enough anyway. It's just that I made a few detours via Bordeaux that's all. I must say you're pretty good at sorting out routes.

Judy Thank you. I have to admit that your enquiries did receive my very special personal attention.

John I'm sure they did. Well, I'd better get off to the hospital and get it over with. It could be a bit tricky. I'm not exactly looking forward to the next part.

Judy No. I'm sure you're not.

John What will you do now?

Judy Go back home, I suppose.

John Don't you think you ought to stay for a while and go and visit Susan in hospital? It might be a wise move.

Judy (*rising*) I'm sorry, John. I simply couldn't. Susan isn't exactly my favourite person as you know, even though she is my sister. There's never been any love lost between us for as long as I can remember. Even so, I couldn't face her, John. I couldn't—knowing what we've done to her, knowing that we've put her into that awful place.

John You're not starting to have regrets, are you?

Judy Of course I have regrets, John. It's a dreadful thing we've done— you must know it is. What sort of a person would I be if I didn't feel that way about it? But I love you, John, and if that was the only way we could get together then—

Act III

John I love you, Judy. I did it for you, don't forget that.
Judy I'm not likely to forget, John.
John You'd better get off home then.
Judy You don't really mind me going, do you? It's just a matter of being patient. We musn't rush things. It would be stupid to spoil everything now, wouldn't it?
John You're probably right. Yes—I'm sure you are. I'll be in touch as soon as I possibly can to let you know how things are going.

As John takes Judy in his arms, the door UL *opens very slowly*

In the meantime, look after yourself. You're very precious to me, Judy.

Susan enters UL

Susan (*as she enters*) That is probably one of the truest statements you've ever made in your whole life, John.

John and Judy separate, Judy moving DR, *John* DL

John Susan!
Susan (*coming down between them*) My God, you're despicable—both of you. All the way from that wretched hospital, I've been sitting in that taxi praying I was wrong. I was hoping against hope that I'd come to the wrong conclusion.
John Susan, I can explain.
Susan I bet you can. You thought you'd fixed me for good this time, didn't you? Oh, it was a clever plan, I'll grant you that much. What's more it almost succeeded. I don't remember much of what happened last night but I do recall being very frightened—terrified in fact. But you'd be surprised what a good night's sleep under sedation can do. When I woke up this morning, I was amazed how clear my mind was. I started thinking it through. Then, suddenly I remembered something about yesterday.
John (*moving nearer Susan*) Look, Susan—you don't know what you're saying.
Susan Don't start that all over again. I know perfectly well what I'm saying. I have never been more certain of anything. I had an idea at the back of my mind that I'd seen that April March woman somewhere before. Then, as I say, I suddenly remembered. It was at Hythe when I went down there with Sybil a couple of years ago. She was staying at the same hotel. I didn't have anything to do with her. I don't think I ever spoke to her but Sybil did and this woman borrowed some money from her. I can't remember how much but I know it was more than Sybil could afford at the time. She promised to pay her back when the banks opened on Monday. But by that time, she'd packed her bags and gone without paying her bill or returning the money. The hotel manager made quite a fuss. You must remember, John, I told you about it at the time. I'm positive it was the same woman. Her hair was a different colour but I'm sure it was her. It was the Australian accent I remember particularly.

John You can't be sure, can you? There are thousands of Australian women in this country. But even if it was the same woman, what does that prove?
Susan What same woman, John? I thought you said there wasn't any woman here last night.
John You're getting me confused.
Susan That makes a change, doesn't it? I thought I was the one who was always confused. Well, shall I go on, John? (*She pauses*) Well, shall I?
John If you must, but I don't see that it's getting us anywhere.
Susan We'll have to see about that, won't we? After I'd remembered where I'd seen her before, I started going over our conversation last night and I realized about the cat.
John The cat?
Susan Yes, you know—dear little Satan.
John What about it?
Susan That's what that woman called it, didn't she?
John I don't—
Susan "Where's Satan?" that's what she said, didn't she?
John She may have done—what if she did?
Susan That's our name for the wretched thing. How the hell did she know what we called it unless somebody had told her?
John This is ridiculous.
Susan Unless you had told her. There's nobody else could have told her, is there? I know I didn't.
John So?
Susan Well then—firstly I knew she was a phoney because of Hythe and Sybil—right? Secondly, I knew you must have met her before yesterday because of the cat's name. Do you follow me?
John Go on.
Susan So then I began to try and fathom out the reason why she had come to this house pretending to be the owner. She obviously wasn't—she knew so little about the locality. Then, it suddenly came to me. I was certain I knew the answer. Shall I tell you what it is, John?
John If you must.
Susan I decided that you'd hired her to come here so that she'd be around when that man—whoever he was—turned up pretending to be you. The idea was that she'd confirm that he was you and then, later on, you would deny all knowledge of them and get me into the state you, in fact, did. Oh, it worked all right. I have to admit it was very clever. First she was here and then she wasn't. Then he was here and then he wasn't. I understand that it's quite an old technique for breaking people down. You missed your vocation, John. You should have worked for one of the Communist countries.
John Look, you're mistaken about—
Susan Oh, no—it was you that made the mistakes, John—stupid mistakes like the name of the cat and so on. Anyway—when I was quite certain that I was right, I began to try to fathom out why you'd gone to all that trouble. It wasn't very difficult.

Act III 53

John You're talking nonsense again, Susan.
Judy What's the use, John? She knows everything.
John Shut up, Judy!
Judy I'm sorry, Susan—I'm sorry.
Susan Sorry! God—my dear little sister! You had to have that money, didn't you? You always were a single-minded, selfish little bitch, weren't you?
Judy How did you know it was me?
John Stop it, Judy. Don't say any more.
Judy What's the point in trying to deny it now? You weren't so very clever after all, were you, John? You and your foolproof plan!
Susan I've suspected for some time now that John had some ulterior motive for all those business trips to the Continent. Then, yesterday, when he pretended to lose his passport—you hadn't really lost it, had you, John? Don't bother to answer, John. You don't need to. Anyway, when your passport appeared to be missing, I looked into your travel wallet and I found the bottom carbons of some airline tickets. Every one of them showed Bordeaux as one of the stopping-off places. You didn't tell me you'd been to Bordeaux, John. I didn't think much about it at the time. God help me, I was too concerned about the loss of your passport. But when I remembered it again this morning, lying there in that hospital bed, it all clicked into place. (*She turns to Judy*) When I telephoned you yesterday I was in a terrible state, I admit. I don't remember much of what I said but I do remember something I didn't say.
Judy What was that?
Susan We've stayed in this house twice before. Both times we came to see you in Bordeaux, didn't we?
Judy Yes.
Susan But you never came here to see us, did you?
Judy No, but I don't see—
Susan When I telephoned you yesterday evening, I didn't give you this address. I did mean to but the money ran out before I could tell you. If you don't know the address, how the hell did you know where to come to? We've never told you anything except that it was near Ribérac, have we?
Judy I don't see—
Susan Don't you? There are hundreds of holiday cottages near Ribérac. That's true, isn't it? (*She pauses*) Isn't it?
Judy Yes, I supose there are.
Susan So, the way I figured it out, John must have given you the address and instructions how to find the place just in case it was necessary for you to come here for any reason—such as things not going exactly to plan. And that was that. I discharged myself from the hospital, rang for a taxi and arrived here to find that I'd been only too right.
Judy (*moving closer to Susan*) Susan, what can I say? I'm sorry. I truly am.
Susan You bloody little fool—you need to be. John doesn't know this—God help me I thought he might not approve—but just before I came

on holiday, I went to see the solicitor who's handling Father's estate. I instructed him to draw up the necessary papers for me to sign, when I came home, handing over half of the inheritance to you. I thought it was the least I could do.

Judy Oh, no!

Susan You didn't know that, did you?

Judy How could I have known?

Susan Of course not. As you say, how could you? Now listen to me, both of you, and listen very carefully indeed.

John Susan, I—

Susan Shut up, John. Just shut up and listen to me for once.

John All right—go on.

Susan Whatever else I do or don't do in the future, there are two things I am determined to do when I get back to England. The first is to make certain, beyond a shadow of doubt, that I remain in the right mental state to come into that inheritance. Understand?

John And the second?

Susan Ah yes—the second. You are listening now, aren't you, John? Well—I am going to see that solicitor the very minute I get home and I'm going to tell him to destroy the papers I asked him to draw up. (*She pauses*) Well John, what have you to say for yourself now, eh?

John I don't know what to say.

Susan I'm sure. Well, my dears, you have each other now, haven't you. And do you know, I think that you just about deserve each other.

Judy But I—

Susan That's all right, Judy—that's all right. You can have him. I give him to you with my compliments. I wish you well of him, Judy—I honestly do. But I'll tell you one other thing. That is all you are ever going to get from me now. That is all you are ever going to get from me for the rest of your lives.

CURTAIN

FURNITURE AND PROPERTY LIST

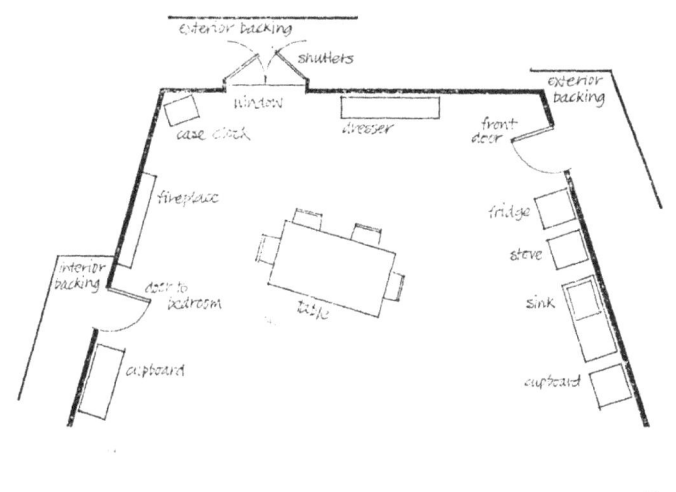

ACT I

On stage: Kitchen table. *On it:* red check cloth
4 upright wooden chairs
Window shutters (closed at start)
On window-ledge: pile of newspapers
Dresser with cupboards. *On it:* plates, bowls, cups, saucers, glasses (one with red grapes painted on it). *In cupboard underneath:* cutlery, coffee-pot, saucepans (including one small green milk saucepan)
Refrigerator (practical)
Calor gas stove (practical). *By it:* box of matches
Sink and taps (practical). *In cupboard under sink:* washing-up liquid, cleaning cloths, plastic bowl, tea-towel, Calor gas bottles
Draining-board
Food cupboard
Long case clock
Stone fireplace with mantelshelf. *On mantelshelf:* 2 gaudy ornaments, a large black stuffed cat
Low cupboard. *On it:* flower vase, pile of paperbacks, photograph in frame, ashtray, brown jug
On walls: prints and pictures
Bolt on door UL (unbolted at start)

Off stage: 2 suitcases (**John**)
Holdall (**Susan**)
Plastic carrier-bag. *In it:* groceries, including coffee, milk, butter, sugar, bread (**Susan**)
Suitcase (**John**)
Radio (**John**)
Leather document case. *In it:* passport, pocket wallet, several airline tickets, other papers (**Susan**)
Bottle of whisky (**John**)
Bottle of brandy (**John**)

Personal: **John:** wrist-watch
Mrs March: handbag. *In it:* coins
Mrs March: wrist-watch

ACT II

Strike: *From table:* 1 dirty glass
Cups, saucers and spoons
½ empty bottle of brandy
Document case
Coins
Stuffed cat
Coffee-pot

Reset: *In cupboard* DL: Green saucepan
Jar of coffee
On dresser: 1 clean glass
Clean cups and saucers
Windows closed
Door UL bolted

Set: Almost-full bottle of brandy on table
Headless stuffed cat covered in blood in cupboard DL

ACT III

Strike: 1 cup and saucer from table
Dirty glasses from table

Reset: Bottle of whisky on dresser

Set: *On table:* Coffee-pot of coffee
Plate of bread and butter
Knife

Check: Door UL bolted

Personal: **Man:** wrist-watch
John: packet of money in inside jacket pocket

LIGHTING PLOT

Practical fittings required: refrigerator, pendant light (with 2 switches)
Interior. A farmhouse kitchen. The same scene throughout

ACT I. Late afternoon

To open: Interior dim; exterior—late afternoon sunshine

Cue 1	As door UL opens *Increase level of light in room*	(Page 1)
Cue 2	**John** opens shutters *Increase level of light as room is bathed in evening sunshine*	(Page 2)

ACT II. Evening

To open: Interior dim, light shining in from bedroom R; exterior twilight

Cue 3	**Judy** switches on main light *Snap on pendant*	(Page 19)
Cue 4	**Man** turns off main light from switch R *Snap off pendant*	(Page 35)

ACT III. Morning

To open: Effect of morning sunlight streaming in room
No cues

EFFECTS PLOT

ACT I

Cue 1	When CURTAIN rises *Clock strikes five, then sound of key being turned in lock*	(Page 1)
Cue 2	**Mrs March:** ". . . managed without." *Car starts up and drives away*	(Page 16)
Cue 3	**Mrs March** slaps coins down on table *Car drives up and stops*	(Page 18)

ACT II

Cue 4	When CURTAIN rises *Clock strikes nine*	(Page 19)
Cue 5	**Judy** exits UL *Pause, then car drives up and stops; car door slams*	(Page 27)
Cue 6	**Judy** (*off*): "See you, John." *Car starts up and drives off*	(Page 34

ACT III

Cue 7	As CURTAIN rises *Radio playing*	(Page 36)
Cue 8	Knock on door UL *Stop radio*	(Page 36)
Cue 9	**Mrs March:** ". . . as far as I'm concerned." *Car drives up and stops*	(Page 46)
Cue 10	**John**, the **Man** and **Mrs March** exit *Car starts up and drives away*	(Page 48)

www.ingramcontent.com/pod-product-compliance
Ingram Content Group UK Ltd.
Pitfield, Milton Keynes, MK11 3LW, UK
UKHW021847210426
5322IPUK00022B/517